CHRIST

AMONG THE

DRAGONS

Finding Our Way Through Cultural Challenges

JAMES EMERY WHITE

IVP Books

An imprint of InterVarsity Press
Downers Grove, Illinois

InterVarsity Press
P.O. Box 1400, Downers Grove, IL 60515-1426
World Wide Web: www.ivpress.com
E-mail: email@ivpress.com

InterVarsity Press® is the book-publishing division of InterVarsity Christian Fellowship/USA®, a
movement of students and faculty active on campus at hundreds of universities, colleges and schools
of nursing in the United States of America, and a member movement of the International Fellowship
of Evangelical Students. For information about local and regional activities, write Public Relations
Dept., InterVarsity Christian Fellowship/USA, 6400 Schroeder Rd., P.O. Box 7895, Madison, WI
53707-7895, or visit the IVCF website at <www.intervarsity.org>.

All Scripture quotations, unless otherwise indicated, are taken from the Holy Bible, New
International Version®. NIV®. Copyright ©1973, 1978, 1984 by International Bible Society. Used
by permission of Zondervan Publishing House. All rights reserved.

Design: Cindy Kiple

Cover images: Four types of dragon (engraving) by English School (19th century). Private Collection/
The Bridgeman Art Library.

Interior image credits and permissions are listed on page 189.

ISBN 978-0-8308-3312-2

Printed in the United States of America ∞

Library of Congress Cataloging-in-Publication Data

White, James Emery, 1961-
   Christ among the dragons: finding our way through cultural
challenges / James Emery White.
      p. cm.
   Includes bibliographical references.
   ISBN 978-0-8308-3312-2 (hardcover: alk. paper)
   1. Evangelicalism.   2. Christianity and culture.   I. Title.
BR1640.W49 2010
261—dc22

                                                                   2010008327

P   22   21   20   19   18   17   16   15   14   13   12   11   10   9   8   7   6   5   4   3   2   1

Y   28   27   26   25   24   23   22   21   20   19   18   17   16   15   14   13   12   11   10

To Billy Graham

CONTENTS

ACKNOWLEDGMENTS

I wish to thank the InterVarsity Press team for their continued support of my life and ministry. That truly is what they are about. So thanks again to my long-time (or is it long-suffering?) editor Cindy Bunch, along with Jeff Crosby and, of course, Bob Fryling. And this time, thank you all for your extreme patience and grace.

I have been greatly blessed by the support of my assistant, Ms. Glynn Goble, for many years. And thanks also need to go out to her husband, Bill, who selflessly allows her to pursue this ministry. Thanks, buddy. And to Alli Main goes special thanks for her hard work and dedication on this project.

I have never failed to mention my wife, Susan, in any book, and for good reason. We are now more than halfway through our third decade of marriage, and for that I am truly grateful to God. She continues to make every page I write, every talk I give, possible.

And to my four children—Rebecca, Rachel, Jonathan and Zachary. May you find your way not simply in faith but in faithfulness. I hope my generation passes the baton well to you, and that you then run fast and free.

In the past I have often ended such opening pages with the

Latin phrase *soli Deo gloria* (to God alone be the glory). Due to a wide and still to me curious chain of events that disrupted my "book a year" rhythm, I offer a different phrase that was common during the medieval era. During that time, when a student would rent or borrow a book, it was for the purpose of copying it to add to their library, but it took long hours and was an arduous task. For that reason, when we survey such works in libraries such as Oxford's Bodleian, we find written across the bottom of the last page *Explicit, Deo Gratias.*

"Finished, thank God."

INTRODUCTION

*At the approach of danger there are always two voices that speak with
equal power in the human soul: one . . . tells a man to consider the nature
of the danger and the means of escaping it; the other . . . says that it is too
depressing and painful to think of the danger . . . and it is therefore better to
disregard what is painful till it comes, and to think about what is pleasant.*

LEO TOLSTOY

What do you write on a map when you come to the end of
the world as you know it? Three words were used by the medieval cartographer of the famed Lenox Globe (c. 1503-1507) to
describe the outer boundaries where knowledge ended and
speculation began:

Hic sunt dragones. "Here be dragons."

After drawing on all of his knowledge, the mapmaker could
only write those three provocative words to convey that these areas were at best unexplored, and at worst, perilous. Yes, such vistas hold great promise, but without a way to navigate, a sense of
"true north," such areas were unmistakably fraught with danger.

Figure I.1. The Lenox Globe, c. A.D. 1503-1507

At the beginning of the twenty-first century, evangelical Christians in America have an equally unsettling map. Reporter David Kirkpatrick penned a cover story for the *New York Times Magazine* with the provocative question "End Times for Evangelicals?" emblazoned on its front, followed by these teaser lines: "They don't have a natural presidential candidate. They don't have. a unified leadership. They no longer seem to share even the same political beliefs."

The actual title of the article is "The Evangelical Crackup."

Many of the evangelical institutions themselves are still relatively robust. What is faltering is the foundation on which they had been established, namely, a shared approach to truth, a joint sense of cultural engagement, a commitment to unity, and a deep commitment to and understanding of the church. Younger evangelicals are straying from core ideas, such as bibli-

yes there is ~~*but it is*~~ *a different* [handwritten annotation]

cal inerrancy; core issues, such as opposition to abortion or gay marriage; and core alliances, such as the National Association of Evangelicals. Simply put, there is no longer a shared core. Truth is increasingly accepted as relative, an emphasis on social justice is rapidly supplanting previously focused concerns on social morality, relational and missional networks are becoming more generational in makeup, and older models of church and parachurch are being replaced with emerging communities that tend to defy traditional ecclesiastical standards.

A few evangelical leaders, such as Charles Colson, took the article to task in its portrayal of older evangelicals as distanced from core social issues, noting his own work in prisons, Focus on the Family's James Dobson and his work with families, and Moral Majority leader Jerry Falwell and his work with unwed mothers. The evangelical mosaic, he argued, is still united in its efforts to uphold traditional values, defend life, and pursue justice and care for the poor.

But few joined Colson in speaking out against the article. Kirkpatrick placed a finger on the pulse of evangelical Christianity by highlighting the real and growing divide "over the evangelical alliance with the Republican Party, among approaches to ministry and theology, and between the generations." Further, he noted the passing of many of the founding leaders of the 1980s era who first guided evangelicals into the political arena, such as Jerry Falwell and James Kennedy. And Billy Graham? While still alive at the time of this writing, the Pew Forum on Religion and Public Life discovered that nearly one out of every three Americans under the age of thirty has never even *heard* of Billy Graham. In one of his most deft observations, Kirkpatrick makes the following assessment:

Meanwhile, a younger generation of evangelical pastors—

including the widely emulated preachers Rick Warren and
Bill Hybels—are pushing the movement and its theology
in new directions. There are many related ways to characterize the split: a push to better this world as well as save
eternal souls; a focus on the spiritual growth that follows
conversion rather than the yes-or-no moment of salvation;
a renewed attention to Jesus' teachings about social justice
as well as about personal or sexual morality. However
conceived, though, the result is a new interest in public
policies that address problems of peace, health and poverty—problems, unlike abortion and same-sex marriage,
where left and right compete to present the best answers.

Such assessments are not necessarily to be disparaged, much
less met with alarm. We should welcome a broadening of traditional evangelical emphases to be more holistic and inclusive.
Also older Christians have much to learn from younger Christians. There is a great need for reverse mentoring. And unexplored territory does not always hold the peril of dragons; it can
also hold the promise of a new world. The concern is a new
fragmentation that leaves evangelicals bereft of their moorings
and unable to speak with a single voice to the world's great
questions, which is the beginning of the loss of evangelical
identity itself.

ON BEING EVANGELICAL

I recall a lunch in graduate school where a fellow doctoral student asked me how he could get networked with evangelicals
and the wider evangelical world. His background was almost
entirely within a denomination that was an island unto itself,
but he knew that I had become a Christian through an evangelical parachurch group in college, was familiar with various

evangelical leaders and was writing my doctoral dissertation on the subject of evangelical theology. In other words, the rumor on campus was that I was one.

I remember feeling somewhat flatfooted in my response. I reflected on how deep my sense of identity ran; what came to mind was that an evangelical was just something you *were*, not an orbit you entered or collection of relationships you networked yourself into. It was akin to being raised in the South. You either were or were not a Southerner. You either drank your iced-tea sweet, had a pig-pickin' instead of a clam bake, called lunch "dinner" and dinner "supper," understood that *barbecue* was a noun, and knew how to shag on the beach—and knew that meant a *dance*—or you didn't.

I just knew I *was* a certain type of Christian—and knew what it meant to *be* that kind of Christian. I looked to Billy Graham for inspiration and C. S. Lewis, Francis Schaeffer and John Stott for intellectual guidance. I believed the Bible to be true from Genesis to the maps in the back and the Scofield notes on the bottom. Thanks to Hal Lindsey and Salem Kirban, I thought the rapture had taken place every time I came home to an empty house. And, of course, I went to Christian camps every summer where, also every summer, I rededicated my life. Or at least tried to. I didn't actually give my life to Christ until college—but even then, it was in a thoroughgoing evangelical way: through a campus evangelical parachurch ministry.

Not every Christian shares this world, I know, but those of us that did, by and large, made up the kind of Christian I knew I was.

So I told him a few things, and some folks he might connect with. I doubt I was of much help. But he ended up networking quite well, and now serves as a seminary president and is on the board of many evangelical groups.

I suppose he joined the ranks.

Of course, evangelicalism is much more than this. David Bebbington captures the heart of its moorings as well as any: conversionism, activism, biblicism and crucicentrism. Big words, but simple ideas. *Conversionism* is the belief that an individual's life must be transformed. *Activism* is the conviction that we must not be passive when it comes to the gospel, but active in our expression, proclamation and application. *Biblicism* captures our high regard for the Bible—we go *to* the Bible, and then we go *with* the Bible. And *crucicentrism* is the emphasis on the sacrifice of Christ on the cross. "Together," Bebbington concluded, we have "a quadrilateral of priorities" that forms "the basis of Evangelicalism." And, many would add, the basis of the gospel.

Part of the dilemma is that of late, these four marks have faced tension within evangelical ranks. Historian Mark Noll notes that while

> reliance on Scripture remains, . . . how that reliance is expressed differs widely. . . . Concern for conversion also remains, though conversion is understood differently in, for example, charismatic, confessional, or Baptist circles. . . . Evangelicals are as active as ever, but that activity spreads over every point on the compass. . . . Finally, the death of Christ on the cross is still at the heart of evangelical religion, although the formal doctrines that once defined the message of atonement receive much less attention today than thirty or sixty or a hundred years ago.

Interestingly, since the time of Noll's assessment, even the "heart of evangelical religion," the atonement, has become the center of heated theological discourse. Not in a renewal of its centrality, but as a flashpoint for ever-increasing evangelical disunity on its primary meaning.

All the more reason why my sense of evangelicalism was a tenuous foundation, at best, for an identity, as it was far more sociocultural than theological. But it *was* a foundation, and it actually felt strong and clear. I knew who our leaders were, the publishers that could be trusted, the schools I should attend. I knew how best to vote, and where to stand on matters of morality. Yet unlike a denomination, there were no centralized headquarters, elected leadership or official creeds. My sense of Christendom enveloped a wide range of theologically conservative Protestants as well as a small but increasing number of Roman Catholics (though we were never quite sure they were "in"). It was held together by a network of communities and organizations, churches and parachurch groups, and most of all through the singular personality and presence of Billy Graham.

Suffice it to say, that era of evangelical faith in America is now gone. Perhaps, in light of our present cultural challenges, it is even best that it is. What some fear is that the heart of evangelicalism itself is also fading.

And fading fast.

THE SILENT CREEP OF IMPENDING DOOM

But how do the once mighty fall?

It was a question that intrigued bestselling business author Jim Collins, whose previous works *Built to Last* and *Good to Great* charted how the mighty *rise*. But it was how some of the greatest companies in history, including some once-great enterprises he had heralded in his previous books, had *fallen* that perplexed his naturally curious mind. What brought the matter to the surface was an invitation to address a group of twelve U.S. Army generals, twelve CEOs and twelve social-sector leaders about "America." Not sure what he would have to offer such an illustrious group, he remembered an old mentor's advice: "Don't try to come up with the right answers; focus on coming up with good questions." After wrestling with the right question, he came up with this: "Is America renewing its greatness, or is America dangerously on the cusp of falling from great to good?"

As you might imagine, half of his students on that day felt that America stood as strong as ever, and half contended that America teetered on the edge of decline. At a break, the chief executive of one of America's most successful companies pulled Collins aside. "I find our discussion fascinating, but I've been thinking about your question in the context of my company all morning," he mused. "We've had tremendous success in recent years, and I worry about that. And so, what I want to know is, *How would you know?*"

That question captured Collins's imagination. *How would you know?* If you were in organizational decline, what would be the signs? What made the question more pressing was Collins's early sense, later confirmed through his research, that decline is analogous to a disease, perhaps like a cancer, that can grow on the inside while we still look strong and healthy on the outside.

He called it "the silent creep of impending doom."

Collins's work raises a significant question for more than just companies or even nations. How do we know if evangelical faith is alive and well, or in decline? What areas demand close inspection to see if we are aligned toward true north or drifting off course?

A POST-CHRISTIAN WORLD

At this point you may wonder why you should care. Most books of spiritual interest deal with personal spiritual formation or the application of biblical principles to core life issues. All well and good. Why leave such comfortable areas and worry about something as seemingly irrelevant and simultaneously overwhelming as the state of evangelical faith? Because it is not irrelevant, and it is precisely its titanic scope that demands our attention, for it is much more pressing than simply evangelicalism.

Fareed Zakaria penned the provocatively titled book *The Post-American World*. His thesis is that there have been two great power shifts of the past five hundred years: the rise of the Western world, and the rise of the United States. His thesis is that we should expect a third shift, the "rise of the rest." The growth of countries such as China, India, Brazil, Russia, South Africa, Kenya and many more is creating a global landscape that is shifting power and allowing wealth and innovation to flourish. As this happens, it will combine with a nationalism that will shape the world for decades. Zakaria notes that America has been concerned with terrorism and immigration, but may be missing the challenge of the new world.

Evangelicals face a similar contest. While many are concerned about the loss of a shared social agenda or the increasing fragmentation of the patchwork mosaic once held together by Billy Graham and the parachurch movement, we are missing our real challenge: not simply a postevangelical America, but a post-Christian world. For this reason getting our bearings as evangelicals is more crucial than at any other point in recent history, if indeed evangelicals bear witness to the gospel and its dynamic.

TRUE NORTH

In what follows I propose some introductory ways to regain our sense of true north in the four arenas that brought us together, and now threaten to drive us apart and leave us bereft of a sense of direction: the nature of truth and orthodoxy, cultural engagement and the evangelistic enterprise, Christian community and civility, and the identity and character of the church.

It is precisely in these four arenas that the contest will be won or lost in regard to not simply having an evangelical presence in our world but a unified Christian witness. Together they will determine whether we are renewing ourselves for a new generation or falling from great to good, or even worse.

Why these four?

Consider truth: Since Pilate's retort to Jesus' claim, the question of truth has been central to the Christian faith. Not simply in terms of whether Christianity itself is true but in what *sense* is it true. And the church: Jesus said that he came to establish his church, and that it would constitute and reflect his ongoing presence—his very body—on earth. And culture? The Great Commission and the cultural commission inherent within it form our principal marching orders. And of course the great high priestly prayer of Jesus as recorded in the Gospel of John made it clear that the truth which has been revealed, embodied by the church and carried to the world would be received only if there was an observable love between those who bear Christ's name.

So pinpointing the nature of truth and orthodoxy, grasping the nature of the church, developing the deepest and most biblical sense of cultural engagement and mission, and fostering love within the Christian community are far more than unique to evangelical faith; they *are* the faith. The four dimensions of our conversation—truth, culture, unity and church—are like the four points of a compass. Together, if properly calibrated and coordinated, they give us a clear sense of direction.

A NEW MAP

It is not difficult to see why medieval cartographers sketched *hic sunt dragones* on the edges of their maps. Yet maps of that era often held another image—Christ. *The Psalter* map (c. 1250), so called because it accompanied a copy of the book of Psalms, featured dragons on the bottom, and Jesus and the angels at the top. Such a map reminds us of the availability of "true north" as followers of Christ.

Yes, there be dragons.

But there is also Jesus and the angels.

And we can follow him—and find our way.

Figure I.2. *The Psalter* map, c. A.D. 1200-1250

TRUTHINESS

THE LOSS OF ABSOLUTES IN A WIKI WORLD

Who's Britannica to tell me the Panama Canal was finished in 1914?
If I wanna say it happened in 1941, that's my right.
I don't trust books. They're all fact, not heart.

STEPHEN COLBERT

There are many ways to chronicle the passing of a year. Consider 2005, the midpoint of the first decade of the twenty-first century: news organizations posted their sense of the top stories, such as Hurricane Katrina, the election of Joseph Ratzinger as Pope Benedict XVI, the war in Iraq, Supreme Court openings, rising oil prices and the London bombings. Some framed the year in view of those who died, such as Pope John Paul II, Simon Wiesenthal or Rosa Parks. Others looked to the top Google searches for insight, which revealed a year filled with interest in XBox 360, *American Idol* and Harry Potter.

Often overlooked, however, are the new words a year brings, this despite Aristotle's reminder that words are "signs of ideas." All the more reason to have paid attention to the annual exercise of the editors of the *Oxford American Dictionary* as they picked their "Word of the Year." For 2005 it was *podcast*. Runners-up included *bird flu, persistent vegetative state* and *sudoku*. Yet in an interview on National Public Radio's *Morning Edition*, editor in chief of the Oxford dictionary, Erin McKean, was asked about words they were watching—words that were bursting on to the scene and might be candidates for coming "Word of the Year" recognition. One of the primary words she noted was telling: *truthiness*.

And it did become the editor's next pick for word of the year.

The word itself is not actually new. It can be found in the *Oxford English Dictionary*. It simply became new culturally, having been reinserted into our lexicon through the Comedy Central television network, and specifically through the premiere of *The Colbert Report* with Stephen Colbert:

> And that brings us to tonight's word: truthiness.
>
> Now I'm sure some of the Word Police, the wordanistas over at Webster's, are gonna say, "Hey, that's not a word." Well, anybody who knows me knows that I'm no fan of dictionaries or reference books. They're elitist. Constantly telling us what is or isn't true, or what did or didn't happen. Who's *Britannica* to tell me the Panama Canal was finished in 1914? If I wanna say it happened in 1941, that's my right. I don't trust books. They're all fact, not heart.

The idea behind *truthiness* is that actual facts don't matter. What matters is how we feel, for we as individuals are the final arbiters of truth. *Truthiness* is the bald assertion that we not only discern truth for ourselves *from* the facts at hand, but also create truth for ourselves *despite* the facts at hand.

Which brings us to another word, *wikiality*, once again courtesy of Mr. Colbert.

Among the Internet's most popular sites is Wikipedia, the online encyclopedia, which is written entirely by unpaid volunteers. Though praised for "democratizing knowledge" by such luminaries as Stanford University law professor Lawrence Lessig, Wikipedia has more than its fair share of detractors. In 2006 the site drew unwanted attention when journalist John Seigenthaler exposed gross errors and fabrications in the biographical entry on his life. Numerous scholars have voiced concern that the encyclopedia is an unreliable research tool and lament students' use of the resource. A paper by a University of California, Merced, graduate student revealed many of Wikipedia's flaws, including often indifferent prose and some serious problems with accuracy. Yet Wikipedia, it would seem, is here to stay. In 2009 the fifth annual Wikimania (a three-day discussion of the Wikimedia Foundation's various projects) was held in Buenos Aires, Argentina. The English-language version of the encyclopedia surpasses one million articles, and the site has become one of the Web's twenty most popular destinations.

Figure 1.1. Stephen Colbert at the 2008 Primetime Emmy Awards

Regardless of the accuracy of certain articles, and separate from the movement advocating free access to information online, Stephen Colbert put his finger on the real issue with his word play. *Wikiality* is defined as "reality as determined by majority vote," such as when astronomers recently voted Pluto off their list of planets. Colbert notes that with Wikipedia, any user can log on and change any entry, and if enough users agree, it becomes "true." Though they have had to tighten this approach up a bit recently, Colbert muses about a wikiality where this could apply to the entire body of human knowledge. "Together we can create a reality we can all agree on. The reality we just agreed on." So through a new wikiality, we can take our collective "truthiness" and make it "fact" for all through majority vote.

With such democratization of knowledge comes the democratization of truth, resulting in an evolution of the idea that "what is true for you is true for you, and what is true for me is true for me" to the new idea that "what is true for us is true for us." And there would be no reason not to hold to its corollary, which would be "and what is true for them is true for them." In a wiki world, there is no truth outside of what the majority determines. Fifty-one percent becomes the final arbiter of reality. The idea of truth is finally divorced from its mooring—it simply drifts along the breezes of cultural mores. Or as Marshall Poe observed in the *Atlantic:* "If the community changes its mind and decides that two plus two equals five, then *two plus two does equal five.*"

THE BANISHMENT OF TRUTH

Beyond the subjectivity of truth, there is also the banishment of truth. The National Academy of Sciences, the nation's most eminent scientific organization, produced a book on the evidence supporting the theory of evolution (and arguing against the introduction of creationism or other religious alternatives in public school science classes) in 1984. It published another in 1999. In 2008, it produced a third, but with a twist; it was intended specifically for the lay public. Further, it devoted a great deal of space to an explanation of the differences between science and religion, maintaining that the acceptance of evolution does not require abandoning belief in God. Barbara A. Schaal, a vice president of the academy, an evolutionary biologist at Washington University and a member of the panel that produced the book, said to the *New York Times*, "We wanted to produce a report that would be valuable and accessible to school board members and teachers and clergy." Titled "Science, Evolution and Creationism," the seventy-page work asserts that "attempts to pit science and religion against each other create controversy where none needs to exist."

So far, so good. While I am not convinced of all that has been suggested under macro-evolutionary theories, and even less those pertaining to hominid evolution, I have no problem with those who hold to various forms of theistic evolution. If, in the end, it is demonstrated that this is the method God chose to use, so be it. The Genesis narrative does not speak to *how* God created, only *that* God created. The Christian has nothing to fear from science because the God of the Bible is the God of creation. All true scientific discoveries simply illuminate the world God has made. But this is not what was meant by the report's desire to diffuse the tension between science and religion. Instead, faith is upheld by trivializing it, reducing it to the likes of a favorite color or preferred style of music. As the report phrased it, science and religion deal with two different kinds of human "experience," that which can be validated as fact (science), and that which can be embraced only in faith (religion). So believe what you want about God—that is your prerogative —just don't treat it like you would a scientific reality.

Granted, modern science is based on empirical evidence and testable explanation. We cannot put God in a test tube

and determine his existence. But there is more at hand here
than science doing its job and knowing its limitations in regard to matters of faith. It *limits* what religion can say about
science. The idea is that we can maintain our religious faith
and our scientific discoveries *not* by seeing both as operating
in the realm of public truth—to be jointly engaged and inter-
preted accordingly—but by seeing them as separate categories
that should never be allowed to intertwine. If we wish to believe in God, fine; just don't posit that this God actually *exists*
as Creator, or that he could be the explanation of anything. As
Ronald Numbers wrote, "Nothing has come to characterize
modern science more than its rejection of appeals to God in
explaining the workings of nature." Hence the report's cate-
gorical rejection of *all* forms of creationism, including intel-
ligent design—calling such positions devoid of evidence, dis-
proven or simply false.

At issue here is the larger cultural current of privatization,
which is the process by which a chasm is created between the
public and the private spheres of life, and spiritual things are
increasingly placed within the private arena. So when it comes
to things like business, politics or even marriage and the home,
personal faith is bracketed off. The process of privatization, left
unchecked, makes the Christian faith a matter of personal preference, trivialized to the realm of taste or opinion. Yet faith
does not simply have a new home in our private lives; it is no
longer accepted *outside* of that sphere. More than showing poor
form, talk of faith has been effectively banished from the wider
public agenda.

So the National Academy of Sciences is happy for religion to
exist, and does not want anyone to see a conflict between science and religion. But do not think this means that those with
religious conviction should pursue science with a religious

worldview on equal footing as those who engage it with a naturalistic perspective.

No, science and religion are encouraged to coexist—as long as religion knows its place.

Which is no place at all.

WHAT IS TRUTH?

If evangelical Christians have trumpeted anything throughout history, it has been truth. Through the heresy-addressing gatherings of the great councils during the patristic era, the *ad fontes* (back to the sources) cry of the Reformation, the bold proclamation of the gospel during the great awakenings or the gauntlet of revelation thrown down before modernism, truth has been our bulwark.

But what do we mean by truth? If we, as Christians, cannot determine the answer to this question, all is lost, for the heart of our faith is the proclamation of the One who is not simply the way or the life, but the *truth*. Yet this is precisely what increasingly plagues us: what *is* truth? Are we subtly succumbing to "truthiness," and thus actively reexamining what we mean by truth as never before?

There have been three major conceptualizations of truth throughout the history of Western thought. The first, and most dominant, has been the correspondence theory of truth. The idea is simple: If I say, "It is raining," then it either is or is not raining. A person can walk outside to discover whether my statement corresponds with reality. This is by far the most common understanding of the nature of truth, and has left the strongest mark on evangelical theology. Of course, its weakness is that not everything can be verified by going outside. I might say, "There is a God." Open the door—is my statement proven?

However, the greater dynamic of the correspondence theory is that whether we can validate something or not, what is true is that which does indeed correspond with reality—regardless of our current ability to actually *make* that correspondence. So while a triune God may not be discernible through the empirical method of science, the correspondence idea is that the triune God is true because there is, indeed, a triune God who exists in reality. This may take faith to embrace, but the faith is that this triune God corresponds with reality. If we could conduct an experiment that validated God's existence, we would find him very much validated. To discount correspondence as a theory for truth because we cannot empirically verify everything is highly suspect, for that would make the empirical method the final determinant of all that *is*—or more to the point, it would elevate our five senses as the sole determinant of not simply truth but reality.

A second theory regarding the nature of truth is the coherence theory, which is the idea that truth is marked by coherence—meaning a set of ideas that do not contradict each other. The coherence theory of truth is much like a Sudoku puzzle. The numbers must align; there can't be a violation of the internal rules; the completed puzzle must fill in all of its own squares. Imagine a system of thought, consisting of a tightly bound set of ideas that, when introduced, complement one another and hold no internal contradictions. Perhaps you might think of the ideas as a set of colors that do not clash when put side by side. The coherence theory of truth holds that truth is not only coherent but ultimately is a system of thought that "hangs together" in a superior way to *other* systems of thought. So one political theorist might consider democracy as "truer" than Marxism in terms of its internal consistency.

The dilemma is that such a view divorces itself from what may, in fact, be true. Think of the testimony of a witness during a trial: the story may make sense, and "hold up" under cross-examination. But that doesn't make it true. The argument simply presents itself as a plausible narrative without internal contradiction. Granted, this is far better than contradicting itself. But it still is not sufficient. Further, the Bible goes out of its way to suggest that a coherence view of truth can—and will—prove grossly inadequate when it comes to the things of God, as it records God saying "my thoughts are not your thoughts, / neither are your ways my ways" (Isaiah 55:8), and contends that the gospel itself can seem "foolish" to the human mind (1 Corinthians 1:18-25). Thus a human perspective will always find aspects of God's truth incoherent, though it remains profoundly true.

A third major contender for the idea of truth is the pragmatic theory of truth. When someone is being pragmatic, they are pursuing a course of action because it achieves an end result. So a pragmatic theory of truth maintains that something is true if it works. This is an appealing view, particularly when we consider Jesus' words that we are to judge things by their fruit. However, determining what is truly fruit of the Holy Spirit, and what is done in the flesh—or even what is, in the end, evil—is tricky business. One need only think of the "final solution" of Nazi Germany. Hitler believed that the principal woes of Germany were found in the Jewish people. They constituted an "erosion of capital" and a "waste of space." From this, the removal of "lebensunwertes Leben" (life unworthy of life) was elevated to the highest duty of medicine. "Of course I am a doctor and I want to preserve life," maintained one Nazi doctor. "Out of respect for human life, I would remove a gangrenous appendix from a diseased body. The Jew is the gangrenous appendix in the body of mankind." As a result, the "final solution" was their extermination. There can be little doubt of the workmanlike efficiency evidenced by the smoke which billowed from the furnaces of Auschwitz, yet there have been few enterprises more uniformly condemned as untrue—as well as rank evil.

So among the three candidates competing for our best understanding of truth, it would seem that the correspondence theory deserves its place of prominence in Christian and, more broadly, Western thought. But this is precisely what we seem to be losing, and at risk is our sense of revelation itself.

THE BIBLE AS TRUTH

The idea of revelation is found in the history of the word itself, which is rooted in theater. It referred to the pulling back of a curtain to reveal what was on the stage; if the curtain had *not* been pulled back, the contents would not have been "revealed." In theology, of course, God pulls back the curtain. Playing off of this history, theologian William Hendricks writes, "He draws back the curtain to reveal the central plot of the drama of life's meaning. . . . This script cannot be discovered. It must be revealed. The drama unfolds. God opens the curtain."

But what has been revealed?

There is little debate among evangelicals that God is truth, in terms of moral attributes. He cannot lie; he is genuine, authentic. He is what he appears to be. Further, this God of integrity has revealed himself, truth about himself, to us through revelation. Further, in the Bible we have a record of much of that revelation—inspired and preserved by the Holy Spirit for our lives. It is the *nature* of that truth that is at issue.

To be fair, many question the correspondence view of truth less for its validity than as a result of its often wooden and unsophisticated presentation. They look at the Bible and feel that a strict correspondence view of truth leaves the Scriptures bloodless and our personal interaction and response more cerebral than transformative.

Consider the idea of biblical inerrancy, which holds that the Bible is "truth without mixture of error," the absence of error meaning that it passes the correspondence test for truth. If the

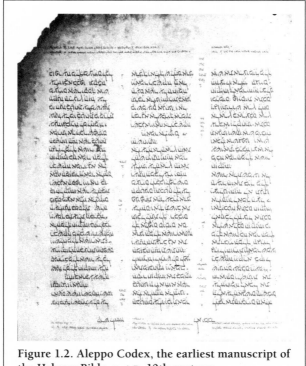

Figure 1.2. Aleppo Codex, the earliest manuscript of the Hebrew Bible, c. A.D. 10th century

Bible says that the sea parted, an ax head floated and a prison gate opened, it did. Yet, as one of my students wrote on his test when answering a question related to the inerrancy of Scripture, "It's a stupid word, and a stupid idea." What he meant by "stupid" is that it seemed to him an imposed category of thought, more Aristotelian than Hebraic, which did not fit the actual dynamic of the Scriptures.

He got the "Hebraic" part from me.

I often teach my students, at the risk of gross oversimplification, that there are three primary ways of looking at reality, at least among those of us in the West. First, there is the Greek way, which is largely descriptive and explanatory. The Greek way of looking at the world has an emphasis on rationality. Aristotle, for example, felt that once we define something, we have exhausted its essence. When we approach something with Greek questions, we tend to be searching for shape and substance and definition. So we might approach water and ask, *What* is water? What does it *look* like? What does it *feel* like? A second way of looking at reality could be termed the Latin way, which is primarily concerned with method. A Latin would ask, How does this *work*? In terms of theology, a Latin question might be, *How* is one saved?

Greek and Latin questions are the currency of our intellectual economy. The problem is that we can't always ask Greek or Latin questions of the Bible because it's not a Greek or Latin book. The New Testament might have been written in Greek, but except for aspects of the apostle John's strategy in the Fourth Gospel, it was not written from a Greek philosophical orientation. Which brings us to a third way of approaching reality— the Hebraic. The Hebrew mind was concerned with what a thing is for, and does it work. Matters of use, utility and value were paramount. This is why we can read all four Gospels of the life and teaching of Jesus and never once find a physical description of Jesus. To the Hebrew mind, it simply wasn't important. So when the Old Testament says that an angel visited, the question was not "What did he look like?" but "What does he want us to do?"

One of our great challenges is that we often come to the Bible with Greek and Latin questions that it simply doesn't answer because it's not a Greek or Latin book. Granted, such questions appeal to us because they are often *our* questions. Those of us from the West tend to come to the Bible with a modernist, Enlightenment set of assumptions and expectations. Yet it is a Hebrew book framed from a Hebrew mindset. So when we read Genesis and want to know *how* God created the world, we are never told. The narrative simply tells us that God did it, and it was good. When we superimpose our Western, Enlightenment questions on a Hebrew text that is largely storied in content, we fall short of capturing the full nature of its truth.

But this does not negate the importance of holding to a correspondence understanding of truth as much as it raises the challenge of contending for that truth and helping others engage it for their lives. Instead of abandoning the correspondence view, we must instead help those who ask Greek and Latin questions of the Christian faith to grapple with what will inevitably be deeply Hebrew and personally life-changing answers, which is the power of the Hebrew worldview. Further, we must refrain from giving Greek and Latin answers to those who are wrestling with deeply Hebrew questions, which creates angst regarding the concept of truth. For the angst of many has less to do with truth itself, or the Bible as truth, as it does with how to most appropriately read the Bible *as* a truth source. It should go without saying that we interact with a particular biblical text in light of the nature of truth it intends to convey. And we should beware of bringing questions to bear that never entered the author's mind or would do violence to the intent of the text itself. The truth we find might be poetic in nature, it might be propositional or didactic in nature, or it

may demand a personal response. Yet it is *all* truth and ultimately should be seen as corresponding with reality.

We must also understand that the Word of God is primarily
that which points to a Person, which means that truth is not to
be understood only in terms of correspondence but dynamic
response, obedience and effectiveness are just as decisive. These
are important corollaries to the idea of the truth of the Bible.
An overly rationalistic approach to interpretation obscures the
mysterious, the transcendent, the paradoxical and the aesthetic.
This does not mean that God or his revelation is nonrational
but rather suprarational; God is larger than our reason. So is
truth rational? Certainly, but that is not *all* that truth is, and
rational thought is not all there is to say about truth. Human
language and thought cannot exhaustively contain the truth of
God. All truth corresponds with reality, but not all of reality
corresponds with human rationality.

Yet such talk of correspondence runs the risk of reducing the
challenge of truth to a philosophical debate. In practice, it is
more experiential than philosophical. In a "truthy" world, it
seems natural to approach the Bible in a similarly "truthy" way.
But an experiential approach has a darker side: the rejection of
the *authority* of truth. It is a seduction that is as old as temptation itself: "Did God *really* say . . . ?" If we wish to liberate ourselves from the authority of God's truth, the simplest maneuver
is to change the *nature* of that truth. As a pastor, I have learned
that when people tell me they reject some of the principal truths
of the Christian faith, my best response is to probe more deeply
into their personal life. Or as one of my more direct pastor
friends puts it, "Tell me about your sex life." More often than
not, there is moral rebellion taking place that is served by making the clear truths of Scripture much more ambiguous than
they are.

Lee Strobel exposed this masterfully in his imagined tale of a daughter and her boyfriend going out for a Coke on a school night. The father says to her, "You must be home before eleven." It gets to be 10:45 and the two of them are still having a great time. They don't want the evening to end, so suddenly they begin to have difficulty interpreting the father's instructions:

> What did he really mean when he said, "*You* must be home before eleven"? Did he literally mean us, or was he talking about *you* in a general sense, like people in general? Was he saying, in effect, "As a general rule, people must be home before eleven"? Or was he just making the observation that "Generally, people are in their homes before eleven"? I mean, he wasn't very clear, was he?
>
> And what did he mean by, "You *must* be home before eleven"? Would a loving father be so adamant and inflexible? He probably means it as a suggestion. I know he loves me, so isn't it implicit that he wants me to have a good time? And if I am having fun, then he wouldn't want me to end the evening so soon.
>
> And what did he mean by, "You must be *home* before eleven"? He didn't specify *whose* home. It could be anybody's home. Maybe he meant it figuratively. Remember the old saying, "Home is where the heart is"? My heart is right here, so doesn't that mean I'm already home?
>
> And what did he really mean when he said, "You must be home before *eleven*"? Did he mean that in an exact, literal sense? Besides, he never specified 11 p.m. or 11 a.m. And he wasn't really clear on whether he was talking about Central Standard Time or Eastern Standard Time. In Hawaii, it's still only quarter to seven. As a matter of fact, when you think about it, it's *always* before eleven. What-

ever time it is, it's always before the next eleven.

So with all of these ambiguities, we can't really be sure what he meant at all. If he can't make himself more clear, we certainly can't be held responsible.

More often than not, this is how evangelicals who whole-heartedly embrace a Savior who claimed to be "the truth" reject the authority inherent within that truth. And why are we so prone to this? Ironically, it may be due to the great hallmark of evangelicalism itself—namely, the celebration and promulgation of a "personal relationship" with Christ, which can reduce Christianity to little more than personal experience, making Jesus and the Christian experience whatever we most desire.

This was reflected comically in the movie *Talladega Nights*. During a meal-time prayer, race-car driver Ricky Bobby, played by Will Ferrell, decided he wanted to pray to baby Jesus, which opened the door to an interesting theological discussion between Ricky Bobby, his son, his wife Carley, her father and Ricky Bobby's best friend Cal.

RICKY BOBBY: Dear Tiny Infant Jesus . . .

CARLEY: Hey, umm, you know sweetie, Jesus did grow up. You don't always have to call him "baby." It's a bit odd and off-puttin' praying to a baby.

RICKY BOBBY: I like the Christmas Jesus best and I'm saying grace. When you're saying grace, you can say it to grown-up Jesus, or teenage Jesus, or bearded Jesus, or whoever you want.

Dear Tiny Jesus, with your golden-fleeced diapers, with your tiny little fat balled up fists . . .

CARLEY'S FATHER: He was a man. He had a beard.

RICKY BOBBY: Look, I like the baby version the best. Do you hear me? I win the races and I get the money . . .

CAL: I like to picture Jesus in a tuxedo T-shirt. 'Cause it says like, "I want to be formal, but I'm here to party too." 'Cause I like to party so I like my Jesus to party.

SON: I like to picture Jesus as a ninja fightin' off evil Samurai.

CAL: I like to think of Jesus with like with giant eagle's wings singin' lead vocals for Lynyrd Skynyrd with, like, an angel band. And I'm in the front row and I'm hammered drunk . . .

RICKY BOBBY: OK. Dear 8 pound, 6 ounce, newborn Infant Jesus, don't even know a word yet. . . . Thank you for all your power and your grace dear Baby God. Amen.

CAL: That was a hell of a grace, man. You nailed that like a split hog.

RICKY BOBBY: I appreciate that. I'm not gonna lie to you, that felt good.

A comedy, to be sure, but one that reflects a way many approach Jesus. Before long, to borrow from the lyrics of Depeche Mode, we each have our "own personal Jesus," though that Jesus may not be the Jesus of the Bible.

But we may not realize it until we are long past deceived.

TRUTH MATTERS

A Million Little Pieces by author James Frey sold more than 1.7 million copies since Oprah Winfrey selected it for her book club. Only J. K. Rowling's *Harry Potter and the Half-Blood Prince* sold more copies in the United States the year it was released. As cracks in Frey's account of his life began to surface through such investigative websites as *The Smoking Gun*, Frey admitted he lied about past criminality. Arguing that he wrote "the emotional truth," Winfrey defended Frey and called the uproar "much ado about nothing," intimating that the truth of the book mattered less than its story of redemption.

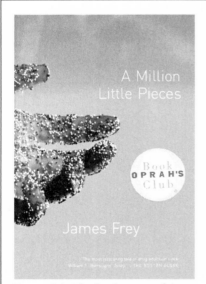

Figure 1.3. The book cover of *A Million Little Pieces* by James Frey

The *emotional* truth? Perhaps that sounded good at first, but not for long. Not even for Oprah.

In a stunning switch from dismissive to disgusted, Winfrey eventually accused Frey on live television of lying and letting down fans of his account of addiction and recovery. "I feel duped," she said on the show. "But more importantly, I feel that you betrayed millions of readers." In discussing her change of mind, Winfrey said, "I left the impression that the truth is not important."

Good for Oprah. Even a skeptic as hardened as Sigmund Freud had to maintain that if "it were really a matter of indifference what we believed, then we might just as well build our bridges of cardboard as of stone, or inject a tenth of a gramme of morphia into a patient instead of a hundredth, or take tear-gas as a narcotic instead of ether." Put another way, it matters whether we have a million little pieces or a million little lies.

A TALE OF TWO LIVES

Where we stand on truth will determine the course of our life, particularly if we consider ourself a follower of Christ. Early in his life Billy Graham wrestled with whether he was going to embrace the Bible as the inspired, revealed Word of God and therefore the ultimate truth source for his life, or view it through eyes that dismissed it as a fallible book of human insight. He intuitively knew that this was no mere intellectual decision, but that it would alter the very trajectory of his life.

Billy's friend Chuck Templeton was facing the same decision. Both were rising stars in the evangelical world, although most considered Templeton the better speaker of the two. But as Templeton looked at the Bible, he made the decision not to believe it, viewing it as little more than any other book. He then tried to convince Billy to take a similar position.

The resolution came while Billy was at a student conference at Forest Home, a retreat center in the San Bernardino Mountains near Los Angeles. Billy went for a walk in the surrounding pine forest. About fifty yards off the main trail, he sat for a long time on a large rock that was there, with his Bible spread open on a tree stump. Then he made his choice, ultimately and finally, praying: "Oh God, I cannot prove certain things. I cannot answer some of the questions Chuck is raising and some of the other people are raising, but I accept this Book by faith as the Word of God."

And that, Billy would later say, changed everything.

I've been to Forest Home, and on a similar walk I accidentally stumbled on the very rock where Graham made his life-long values choice. I knew it was the same rock because there is now a bronze tablet on the stone commemorating his decision. Why such recognition? Because through that decision Graham was used by God to change the world. Graham says that single resolution

> gave power and authority to my preaching that has never left me. The gospel in my hands became a hammer and a flame. . . . I felt as though I had a rapier in my hands and through the power of the Bible was slashing deeply into men's consciousness, leading them to surrender to God.

Sadly, the world never heard any more from Chuck Templeton. He ended up resigning from the ministry and eventually left the faith altogether. He was interviewed at the age of eighty-three, living with Alzheimer's disease. Asked by a journalist about his youthful decision, he reflected back on his life, and said that he missed Jesus.

And then he broke down in tears, and could say no more.

ORTHODOXY

THE DOGMA IS THE DRAMA

It is not our doctrine that we bring you this day; we wrote it not,
we found it not out, we are not the inventors of it; we bring you
nothing but what the old fathers of the church, what the apostles,
what Christ our Savior himself hath brought before us.

JOHN JEWEL (1562)

It stretched 548 feet across the vast, open space of Turbine Hall at Tate Modern in London, the national gallery of international modern and contemporary art. Titled *Shibboleth,* the Colombian sculptor Doris Salcedo created a jagged, open crack down the length of the museum's massive concrete floor. It began small at the top of the slope as a hairline crack, and then widened as it progressed, gaining depth and creating additional, smaller fissures.

The meaning?

Museum literature stated that "a 'Shibboleth' is a custom, phrase or use of language that acts as a test of belonging to a particular social group or class. By definition, it is used to exclude those deemed unsuitable to join this group." Or from the *Oxford English Dictionary, shibboleth* is "a word used as a test for detecting people from another district or country by their pronunciation; a word or a sound very difficult for foreigners to pronounce correctly." To delve further into the title's origins, which the artist freely acknowledges and the museum made known, we must explore the biblical incident recorded in the book of Judges,

> which describes how the Ephraimites, attempting to flee cross the river Jordan, were stopped by their enemies, the Gileadites. As their dialect did not include an "sh" sound, those who could not say the word "shibboleth" were captured and executed. A shibboleth is therefore a token of power: the power to judge, reject and kill. . . . [Salcedo] invites us to look down into it, and confront discomforting truths about our world.

Museum placards went further and explained, "Shibboleth asks questions about the interaction of sculpture and space, about architecture and the values it enshrines, and about the shaky ideological foundations on which Western notions of modernity are built." The idea is that such fractures will, in the end, undermine everything that attempt to rest on it. The point is clear: shibboleths are bad and create division. No one person, much less society, should establish any shibboleths representing what all should embrace, embody or emulate.

Upon seeing *Shibboleth,* I felt something visceral. Like many others, I went down to the main floor, examining the divide, even stepping into the deeper fissures. I resonated with the reviewer in the London *Telegraph* who wrote, "After I left the hall, Shibboleth rattled around in my head all day, and it haunts me still. When I ask myself why, I realize it is because it looks like a wound, a gash that can't heal. It offers no hope, leaving you feeling as empty as the abyss it opens up beneath your feet."

THE HARD SELL OF DOCTRINE

Thus we come to one of the great tensions for those of us who follow Christ—a deep and profound desire to bridge cultural, social, ethnic and geographic divides, while necessarily holding to a defined faith that is, by its very nature, a shibboleth.

I recall an old theology professor in seminary reflecting on his service to the World Council of Churches Faith and Order Commission. He had been involved in a paper on the Unification Church, whose members are known as the Moonies. The conclusion was that the Unification Church was not a Christian sect. He received an irate call from a Moonie saying, "How dare you say we are not Christian! How dare you say whether anything is Christian!" To which he replied, "Madam, if you cannot say what is *not* Christian, you cannot say what *is*."

His point is well-taken. If there is truth, then, as missiologist Lesslie Newbigin made clear in his Osterhaven Lecture, there is "truth to tell." It is not a personal, private truth. If truth is anything, it is public. Truth necessarily shoulders its way into our lives and demands to be accounted for. But this is precisely what is increasingly disliked and rejected. There is a growing disdain for all things "macro," meaning statements which smack of ultimate, objective truth suggesting metanarratives for the world as a whole. As Salcedo's art suggests, it leads only to division and discord, and in the end a collapse of civilization itself. She is not alone in her sentiment. As G. K. Chesterton observed a century earlier,

> General theories are everywhere condemned. . . . We are
> more and more to discuss details in art, politics, litera-

ture. A man's opinion on tram cars matters; his opinion on Botticelli matters; his opinion on all things does not matter. He may turn over and explore a million objects, but he must not find that strange object, the universe. . . . Everything matters—except everything.

Much of this flows from our wholesale embrace of the virtue of tolerance. Unfortunately, we have not been careful with this virtue's true dynamic. When we speak of tolerance, we usually mean social tolerance: "I accept you as a person." Or at times legal tolerance: "You have the right to believe what you wish." We do not, however, tend to mean *intellectual* tolerance. This would mean that all ideas are equally valid. No one believes that ideas supporting genocide, pedophilia, racism, sexism or the rejection of the historical reality of the Holocaust, are to be tolerated. But we find ourselves sloppily embracing the idea of intellectual tolerance under the overarching mantra of "tolerance."

Yet as a Christian I am sympathetic to the seduction. The media has long equated fundamentalism with intolerance, evangelicals with fundamentalist absolutism, and anything related to absolutes with ignorance. It's enough to make any Christian move as far away as possible from anything that even smacks of intolerance—intellectual or otherwise. And some distancing is needed. Many Christians are rightly concerned to part ways with the unnecessary shibboleths that earlier generations of Christians put forward in their often vain attempt to separate from the world, which often did little more than condemn it. But in so doing, we now seem desperate to have our faith find a foothold in cultural acceptance, consciously distancing ourselves from taking a stand on anything culture has caricatured.

This has led to the desire for an ever-widening umbrella under which to stand, so wide that a sense of what the umbrella actually covers is being lost. Some have gone so far as to reject the need for any kind of "statement of faith" altogether. The idea is that Jesus did not have a statement of faith—he was about "calling people into trustworthy community" as opposed to "cognitive assent to abstract propositions." The dilemma with such a position, as T. S. Eliot rightly pointed out, is that "it is not enthusiasm, but dogma, that differentiates a Christian from a pagan society."

When I first started Mecklenburg Community Church, we met in a Hilton Hotel ballroom. We had no property, no money and very few attendees. A woman and her husband began attending during our first few weeks. She was electric—young, attractive, talented. Even better, she seemed spiritually solid. She dropped names of authors like C. S. Lewis that warmed the heart of a church planter in desperate need of volunteers. In the early days, I often joked that the only requirement needed to serve is a pulse. This woman had a pulse and a pedigree. Needless to say, she was fast-tracked into leadership. She was gifted in drama, and we had a vision for the arts, so we used her to begin writing sketches and bringing them to life to enhance the topic of the weekend services.

After several weeks of public services I announced our first membership class. The goal was to explain the church's vision, mission, values and beliefs. As expected, she and her husband registered. It was a formality, of course—they were already an integral and visible part of the team.

The morning class was offered in two sessions, with a short break between. During the break, I was approached by the woman and her husband. They looked very perplexed. Holding the membership notebook in their hand, they had been reading our short statement of faith in the appendix.

"Jim, this says that Jesus was God himself in human form. I mean, *God*. The second person of a trinity. Do you really believe that?"

In a flash, the horror of it all struck me. How I had platformed them; how they had been on stage representing the church. All I could stammer out was, "Yes, don't you?"

And they said, "No, we don't."

I learned an important leadership lesson that day.

Statements of faith *matter*.

OF INCEST AND APES

But statements of faith matter for more reasons than internal integrity. They matter as we seek to engage the most pressing issues of our day, which often rest on the most foundational issues of Christian thought, such as what it means to act appropriately as a human. A recent London *Times* report titled "I Used to Have Sex with My Brother but I Don't Feel Guilty About It" offered a detailed narrative of a woman's sexual relationship with her biological brother from the time of fourteen to nearly thirty, until he met another person and married. Their sexual trysts were revealed as part of a tale of sibling intimacy and friendship that ended with the ubiquitous reasoning that they were not hurting anyone, so why make it so wrong? Her brother, only a year older, never pushed himself on her, and she was a willing participant. The author's lament is that something "so lovely and natural to me would be regarded as abhorrent."

It is not simply a matter of human action but the much larger question of human identity. Consider the news of a Spanish parliamentary committee which adopted resolutions that would give great apes, such as chimpanzees and gorillas, the right to life, freedom from arbitrary captivity and protection from torture. In other words, the same legal rights as humans. The reasoning was based almost entirely on what it means to be human, which, according to the naturalistic philosophy in place in our world, is entirely genetic.

"Chimps . . . share 98.5% of human DNA, making them as genetically close to humans as horses are to zebras," noted an article in *USA Today*. So why not treat man's closest genetic relative with the legal and cultural rights they so genetically deserve? What else, to a naturalistic mind, would there be to consider? At the time of this writing, a court case from Austria is going further, wanting to actually declare a chimp a person so the animal could have a legal guardian and funds for upkeep. Sound absurd? The European Court of Human Rights is now considering an appeal on behalf of a twenty-eight-year-old chimp named Matthew Hiasl Pan. "If Matthew should win," noted one reporter, "the case would set a legal precedent across Europe to treat apes with some of the same rights as people."

Such stories represent just two of the contests facing a Christian's understanding of what it means to be human—namely, the boundaries of accepted sexual expression, and the boundaries of accepted human identity. And it is just such challenges that demand the building and application of doctrine. As historian Bruce Shelley has observed, "Every plank in the platform of orthodoxy was laid because some heresy had arisen that threatened to change the nature of Christianity and to destroy its central faith." But it goes beyond orthodoxy. Without a clear sense of what we ought to believe about such things as human sexuality and human identity, we will have nothing to offer the world it does not already have.

THE NECESSITY OF ORTHODOXY

Perhaps it would be helpful to see the challenge before us as medieval in nature, for in many ways it is. The great tension of the Middle Ages was between prophecy and order. Historian Jeffrey Burton Russell's thesis is that the dynamic of medieval Christianity was the tension between the "spirit of order," which attempted to reform individuals and their institutions, and the "spirit of prophecy," which attempted to transform them, lifting them out of this world and into the world and life of God. It might be said that earlier evangelicals represent the spirit of order, and there is now an emerging sense of the need for the spirit of prophecy. This is all well and good, but in truth we need both. As Russell notes,

> The search for order and the urge to prophecy, the pro-
> gressives who make necessary adjustments and the con-
> servatives who check the tendency to proceed too far or
> too fast, the constitutional structure of the Church and
> the mystics and ascetics who cried down or ignored the
> structure, the orthodox and the heretics—all these oppo-
> sites are necessary.

The challenges of our day demand fresh thinking. There can be little doubt that much of our doctrine has layers of accumulated dust that needs to be blown off and then examined in view of fresh cultural application and life transformation. But this is vastly different than abandoning the nature of orthodoxy itself.

Orthodoxy, from the Greek words *orthos* (straight) and *doxa* (thought), means "right thinking" or "right belief," and has its roots deep in the idea of revelation. To be orthodox, in the largest sense of the word, means to be in alignment with the Christian faith as revealed in Scripture and as conveyed in a heritage. It is telling that the root of *hairesis*, from which we get our word *heresy*, is the idea of "choice"—meaning choosing for oneself over and above the apostolic tradition. Orthodoxy, then, is not something created as much as it is discovered and then adhered to.

For this reason Christian theology has had the task of first determining what is and is not orthodox or Christian. Related to this is a second task, which is to determine what is *decisively* Christian—meaning what ideas, doctrines and principles are *essential* to the Christian faith. In other words, at what point would someone be apostate, having left the faith due to their beliefs? Is it determined by the acceptance of a penal substitutionary view of the atonement or the idea of *Christus Victor?* Does holding to a pretribulation view of the rapture determine fidelity to the "faith once delivered"? How about the doctrine of Jesus as fully God and fully human?

It shouldn't surprise us then that creeds— statements of faith, if you will—go back to the very beginning of the

Figure 2.1. Writers holding the Creed of Nicaea at the first Council of Nicaea in A.D. 325

church, initiated by the simple "Jesus is Lord." The source of the Nicene Creed is the first great Christian council of A.D. 325, the Council of Nicaea. What pulled together around 230 bishops for the first ecumenical or worldwide council of the church? *Orthodoxy*—and specifically, the *meaning* of Jesus' divinity. It was determined that Christ was of the same substance of the Father—not of like or similar substance. The Greek word used in this phrase was *homoousios*, from *homo*, which means "same," and *ousia*, which means "substance." The alternate consideration was *homoiousios*, from *homoi*, which means "similar," and the aforementioned *ousia*. The difference between the two? A single *i*, or iota, the smallest of Greek letters. Edward Gibbon, in his monumental work *The Rise and Fall of the Roman Empire,* quipped that there has seldom been so much energy spent on a single vowel. But the vowel mattered because it defined the very person of Christ, putting forward once and for all that Christ was "very God of very God," clearly summarizing Jesus' own teaching that "I and the Father are one" (John 10:30). It was considered necessary by the earliest of Christ followers, and for very clear reasons. It was not enough to declare allegiance to a vocabulary alone; it was felt, and rightly so, that we needed to agree to a dictionary.

LOSING OUR LANGUAGE

But today even the words themselves are at risk. Consider the word *sin*. In 1973, psychiatrist Karl Menninger published a book with the provocative title *Whatever Became of Sin?* His point is that sociology and psychology tend to avoid terms like *evil*, *immorality* and *wrongdoing*. Menninger detailed how the theological notion of sin became the legal idea of crime and then slid further from its true meaning when it was relegated to the psychological category of sickness. Sin is now regarded as little more than a set of emotions that can be explained through genetics. So something like lust is not a wrong that threatens our own health and the well-being of others; it's simply an emotional urge that is rooted in the need to propagate the human species, fixed in our genes. We've become so uncomfortable with the idea of sin and evil that we've even tried to turn it into a virtue; lust just becomes "sensuality," and anger means being honest with your emotions.

So why not just do away with the word altogether? The latest edition of the *Oxford Junior Dictionary* for children did just that. In a sweeping revision, "crucial words used to describe . . . traditional topics have been stripped . . . in favour of more 'modern' terms." One analyst was more forthcoming, noting that over six editions of the dictionary dating back to the 1970s, there seemed to be an increasing and systematic purging of all words related to Christianity. Among the entries that vanished in the most recent edition: *disciple, saint, abbey, bishop, altar, chapel, christen, monk* and *sin.*

But this is not a loss that is happening in the secular world alone. Consider the National Study of Youth and Religion, conducted from 2001 to 2005 and perhaps the largest research project on the religious and spiritual lives of American adolescents, which found that while the vast majority of U.S. teenagers identified themselves as Christian, the

> language, and therefore experience, of Trinity, holiness, sin, grace, justification, sanctification, church, Eucharist, and heaven and hell appear, among most Christian teenagers in the United States, . . . to be supplanted by the language of happiness, niceness, and an earned heavenly reward.

Principal investigator Christian Smith writes, "It is not so much that U.S. Christianity is being secularized. Rather more subtly, Christianity is either degenerating into a pathetic version of itself or, more significantly, Christianity is actively being colonized and displaced by a quite different religious faith."

But not the kind of faith that is most needed.

When the ten-year anniversary of the Columbine killings took place, we were able to look back with new insight into the event on the morning of April 20, 1999, that forever changed our national consciousness. We have learned that Eric Harris and Dylan Klebold were not goths. They weren't loners. They weren't in the "Trenchcoat Mafia." They were not disaffected video gamers. They hadn't been bullied. The supposed "enemies" on their list had already graduated a year earlier. They weren't on antidepressant medication. They didn't target jocks, blacks or Christians.

They just wanted to kill.

Two seemingly normal, well-scrubbed high school boys went to their school in a prosperous suburban subdivision with the goal to kill thousands. Their bombs didn't work, so they proceeded to kill thirteen classmates and wound another twenty-four. Never again would we say, "It could never happen here." By 2002 the U.S. Secret Service and U.S. Education Department had completed a study on school shooters and found that no single profile fit them all. What is clear is that few simply "snapped" at the time of the attack. They had usually planned it with meticulous detail. Conclusion? "They are rage shootings," says David Osher, a sociologist and vice president at the American Institutes for Research.

And the rage has continued.

Does the name Byran Uyesugi ring a bell? Robert Hawkins? Mark Barton? Terry Ratzmann? Robert Stewart? In an article titled "Why Are Americans Killing Each Other?" Ted Anthony writes that "each entered the national consciousness when he picked up a gun and ended multiple lives." Forty-seven were killed through mass shootings in the month before the Columbine anniversary alone. As Anthony notes, we now live in a society "where the term 'mass shooting' has lost its status as unthinkable aberration and become mere fodder for a fresh news cycle." But then he asks the pivotal question:

"Why are we killing each other?"

The only answer that could be mustered was the loss of the American dream. Eight years of terrorism angst, six years of war in Iraq, months of recession. He lamented that 663,000 lost their jobs in March 2009 and worries how many might be angry about it—and might have a gun. In truth, the answer is found in one of our lost words. In *Explaining Hitler*, Ron Rosenbaum surveys theory after theory regarding the Nazi leader's atrocities. In the end all of his explanations fail to confront the "laughing" Hitler, the bloodthirsty dictator who was fully conscious of his malignancy. He didn't have to kill the Jews; he wasn't compelled by abstract forces. In truth, he chose to, he *wanted* to.

Here was an evil man.

It brings to mind Jean Bethke Elshtain's experience on the first Sunday following the attacks of 9/11. She went to a Methodist church in Nashville. The minister, which she describes as having a kind of frozen smile on his face, said, "I know it has been a terrible week." Then, after a pause, he continued, "But that's no reason for us to give up our personal dreams." She thought, *Good grief! Shouldn't you say something about what happened and how Christians are to think about it?* But then she realized that when we have lost the term *evil* from our theological vocabulary, it is not easy to talk about such a thing.

But a robust and deeply theological discourse on evil was precisely what the world needed to hear at that moment, and would have been uniquely served in hearing. Millions flooded to churches across the nation to hear a word from God, or at least about God, to make sense of the tragedy. Sadly, many were left as empty and lost as before they entered—which is one reason why the millions who came just as quickly left.

I have noticed a growing hunger for deeper engagement with Christian thought from those inside the faith and those outside but open to faith. I have a unique opportunity to observe both sides as the pastor of a church which has close to 80 percent of its growth coming from those who were previously unchurched. For example, one of our most popular services is called "Txt ur ?s." Those in attendance use their cell phones to text in questions that are projected on screens and then answered. If a large number of questions seem to center around a particular topic, it often becomes the focus of a future sermon series. The predominant question of our most recent event was sin, specifically the dynamics of sin in the life of someone wanting to follow, or come, to Christ. It led to an extended series titled "Wicked," which explained who we are when we sin, what sin does to our lives, the holiness of God and the nature of forgiveness. We spent most of our time in the series reliving the drama of Genesis, viewing Adam and Eve as a window into our lives. The hunger for going deep on such things, and knowing what the Bible has to say on the matter, was palpable.

AMNESIA

My own immediate concern is not simply the abandonment of orthodoxy but also the loss of its memory. For example, Francis Schaeffer insightfully noted that when it came to the battle over biblical inerrancy, he was not concerned for the first generation who did not believe in inerrancy. Those who abandoned the Bible as revealed truth that corresponded with reality would still *interact* with the Bible as if it were true. In other words, the ethics of the Bible would still be in force for their life. They might leave orthodox understandings intellectually, but not experientially. But that would last only for a generation; practice soon follows belief.

Consider the following analogy from G. K. Chesterton.

"Suppose that a great commotion arises in the street about something, let us say a lamp post, which many influential persons desire to pull down," Chesterton imagines.

"A Gray-clad Monk . . . is approached upon the matter and begins to say, . . . 'Let us first of all consider, my brethren, the value of Light. If Light be in itself good—'"

Figure 2.2. G. K. Chesterton (1874-1936)

At this point he is knocked down, and the crowd makes a rush for the lamppost, and tears it down. At this, they congratulate themselves on their contemporary practicality.

"But as things go on, they do not work out so easily," Chesterton observes.

Some people have pulled the lamp post down because they wanted the electric light; some because they wanted old iron; some because they wanted darkness because their deeds were evil.

Some thought it not enough of a lamp post, some too much; some acted because they wanted to smash municipal machinery; some because they wanted to smash something. And there is war in the night, no man knowing whom he strikes.

So, gradually and inevitably, today, tomorrow, or the

next day, there comes back the conviction that the Monk
was right after all, and that all depends on what is the
philosophy of Light.

Only what we might have discussed under the gas lamp,
we now must discuss in the dark.

We often attack the vehicle of something as if it is unattached
to what it provides. The idea of truth is bound with the effort to
express and uphold orthodoxy. We may want to tear down the
idea of right thinking, but in so doing we may tear down the light
which it brings, which allows the conversation in the first place.

So before we jettison the lamppost of orthodoxy, perhaps we
should remind ourselves of the value of the light of truth itself.

MERE CHRISTIANITY

Most of us desire "mere Christianity," a term first coined by
the seventeenth-century Anglican writer Richard Baxter and
brought into mainstream evangelical vernacular through C. S.
Lewis. Baxter, a Puritan, lived through the English Civil War
and threw his support behind Oliver Cromwell and the Parliamentary forces. Cromwell summoned Baxter from his
church in Kidderminster, Worcestershire, to help establish
the "fundamentals of religion" for the new government. Baxter complied, but Cromwell complained that Baxter's summary of Christianity could be affirmed by a Papist. "So much
the better," replied Baxter.

As Alan Jacobs writes in his biography of Lewis, Baxter's
challenge was his refusal to allow Christianity to succumb to
the spirit of fashion and sect. He was convinced there was a
core of orthodox Christianity that Puritans, Anglicans and
Catholics all affirmed, and that should have been a source of
peace among them. "Must you know what Sect or Party I am

of?" he wrote in 1680. "I am against all Sects and dividing Parties: but if any will call Mere Christian by the name of a Party, . . . I am of that Party which is so against Parties. . . . I am a CHRISTIAN, a MERE CHRISTIAN, of no other religion."

Jacobs continues:

> If the danger in Baxter's time had been warfare among various kinds of Christians, the danger in Lewis's time was the evaporation of Christianity altogether. Yet Lewis felt that the remedy for the first crisis was also the remedy for the second: if Christianity is embattled and declining, it is all the more important for Christians to put their differences aside and join to sing the One Hymn of the One Church.

As a pastor charged with shepherding a community, I have learned that establishing such things is pivotal to both the health of our community and the strength of our witness. At each new members' class, I speak as plainly as I can about this dynamic tension, putting forward a clear, concise statement of faith around which we ask for unity, but then delineating the areas of freedom. For example, regarding the various views on the end times, I tell people exploring church membership that at Mecklenburg we have folks who are premillennial, amillennial, postmillennial and those who don't know how many *l*s are in the word *millennial!*

And we all get along.

HARVARD AND VERITAS

The power of mere Christianity, wrote Lewis, is not that it replaces existing communions. "It is more like a hall out of which doors open into several rooms." People will eventually want to enter the rooms to find fires and chairs and meals. But if we cannot first lead them into the hall, we will be hard-pressed to bring people into the rooms.

I was reminded of this when I was invited by Christian groups to speak on Harvard University's campus on the provocative question "Is Harvard Still About *Veritas?*" Latin for "truth," *veritas* serves as the school's motto. The event was open to the university at large, and the sponsoring groups had worked hard to ensure their non-Christian friends would be present. From the response, it was a well-chosen topic.

I spoke on the attractions and pitfalls of postmodernism from a biblical worldview. Along the way we traversed widely through culture, discussing YouTube and AOL, Nietzsche and Buddhism. We looked at the worldview behind Martin Luther King's "Letter from a Birmingham Jail" and whether such a missive could be penned today—and if so, would it spark the cultural revolution it did before. My goal was to present a win-

Figure 2.3. Emerson Hall, Harvard

some and compelling case for orthodox Christianity, ending with Jesus' staggering claim to *be* the truth.

Then came the time for questions and answers.

Student after student came forward to strategically placed microphones in order to pose their questions. I braced myself for the fiery challenges I was sure would follow. They never came. Instead, they wanted to deepen their understanding; instead of argument, they wanted to pursue how such a worldview might factor into moral issues of the day. They were interested in the Word of God in view of what it might mean for a *world* of God. They had searching questions about Christianity proper, to be sure, but more about how claims to truth rooted in any faith might play into the wider scope of policy and community. They were hungry to know what such truth would *mean* if indeed it *was* to exist.

This is what we have to offer the world, which it does not already have: Christ's claim to be *the* way, *the* truth and *the* life. In its original context the *veritas* of Harvard's motto was not a mere abstraction but a truth related to the person and work of Christ. Harvard's earliest motto was *Veritas Christo et ecclesiae* or "Truth for Christ and Church." Rather than separating faith and reason, Harvard set out to *integrate* faith and reason.

Truth and orthodoxy must not be abandoned, it must be reclaimed. Dorothy L. Sayers, creator of the fictional Lord Peter Wimsey and his many mysteries, spoke presciently about being

> constantly assured that the churches are empty because preachers insist too much upon doctrine—dull dogma as people call it.
>
> The fact is the precise opposite. It is the neglect of dogma that makes for dullness. The Christian faith is the

most exciting drama that ever staggered the imagination of man—and the dogma is the drama.

Indeed. Because the drama of our lives revolves around the very things that dogma addresses.

- 3 -

THE WORLD WITHOUT US

RENEWING CULTURE WITH THE TRUE,
THE GOOD AND THE BEAUTIFUL

The church has nothing to say to the world
until it throws better parties.

ROB BELL

One of the more intriguing books of late is Alan Weisman's *The World Without Us*. In what the *New York Times* called a "morbidly fascinating non-fiction eco-thriller," Weisman explores humanity's impact on the planet by asking us to envision our earth without us. If every person on the planet were to vanish tomorrow, what would happen to the works of the human race? As the book's front flap details,

> Weisman explains how our massive infrastructure would collapse and finally vanish without human presence. . . . *The World Without Us* reveals how, just days after humans disappear, floods in New York's subways would start eroding the city's foundations, and how, as the world's cities crumble, asphalt jungles would give way to real ones. It

describes the distinct ways that organic and chemically treated farms would revert to wild, how billions more birds would flourish, and how cockroaches in unheated cities would perish without us.

The book prompts a powerful and provocative question for those of us who follow Christ: If all Christian influence were withdrawn from the world tomorrow, what would the results be, and how long would it be before the world knew it? Are Christians necessary for the ongoing vitality of human culture?

Figure 3.1. *The World Without Us* by Kenn Brown and Chris Wren

If we believe the metaphor Jesus uses in the Sermon on the Mount, "You are the salt of the earth" (Matthew 5:13), the spiritual impact of the removal of Christians *should* be as telling as the ecological impact of the withdrawal of the entire human race from the face of the planet.

OF SALT

In Jesus' day salt was a useful and important element, but not for the purpose of adding flavor to food. Without refrigerators or freezers, canned goods or packaging, salt was used to keep food from spoiling. When people had meat that couldn't be eaten right away, they would rub salt into it, which would prevent the meat from going bad. This makes Jesus' metaphor a powerful one. As John Stott writes,

> The notion is not that the world is tasteless and that Christians can make it less insipid, . . . but that it is putrefying. It cannot stop itself from going bad. Only salt introduced from outside can do this. The church . . . is set in the world . . . as salt to arrest—or at least to hinder—the process of social decay. . . .
>
> God intends the most powerful of all restraints within sinful society to be his own redeemed, regenerate and righteous people.

Stott continues by noting the obvious—namely, that this influence is conditional. "For effectiveness the Christian must retain his Christlikeness, as salt must retain its saltness," Stott observes. "The influence of Christians in and on society depends on their being distinct, not identical." Even further, this difference must be applied to what is, in fact, decaying. Unless the salt penetrates the culture, the decay cannot be arrested.

THICK WEBS

As a professor once opined during my graduate school years, culture is the world in which we are born, and the world which is born in us. Or put another way, culture is the world we live in and the world which lives in us: we are talking about *everything*. Culture is the comprehensive, penetrating context that encompasses our life and thought, art and speech, entertainment and sensibility, values and faith. It cannot be reduced to that which is simply economic or political, demographic or technological. Going further, the essence of culture, in regard to its most profound challenge, is that it is a spirit, a perspective on the world. It doesn't simply give a context for our values, it *shapes* our values because it has values in and of itself. It doesn't merely provide the atmosphere for something such as communication—it forms what communication *is* and how it is achieved. Culture alters not only what is said but what is heard—and how.

Sociologist Clifford Geertz has written some of the most penetrating and insightful definitions related to culture, and he has concluded that culture is "thick," meaning that it cannot be reduced to any one thing but is instead an entire way of life. And, he adds, it is largely self-created. Culture is something we invent, create and fashion. Geertz, borrowing from fellow sociologist Max Weber, notes that "man is an animal suspended in webs of significance he himself has spun." Geertz then adds, "I take culture to be those webs."

How does salt interact with thick webs?

Few questions are more critical. It is one thing to hold to truth and maintain a clear sense of orthodoxy. It is another to convey truth to the world in such a way that it arrests moral decay, creates compassion for the poor, brings justice to the oppressed and defends the cause of the widow and orphan. As if this were not enough, we are to do so in the midst of a fast-moving and rapidly evolving culture that presents ever-changing fronts and poses increasingly challenging questions related to faith and ethics. Not surprisingly, the nature of cultural engagement has established some of the more troubling battle lines between Christians and non-Christians, and among Christians themselves.

BEYOND NIEBUHR

Many have turned to H. Richard Niebuhr, who classically outlined the various responses that could be made in light of the interplay between Christ and culture, with such famous typologies as "Christ Against Culture," "Christ of Culture" and "Christ Above Culture." Yet what Niebuhr actually explained is how two authorities—namely Christ and culture—compete with each another. But the interplay of Christians and culture is less about competing authorities than it is active engagement. In other words, it is one thing to speak of *Christ*'s relationship to culture and something altogether different to speak of *Christians* as transformative agents *within* that culture. Yet as Christians it is our strategy for engagement that is most at hand and in need of examination, because we are losing the cultural challenge. As Alan Wolfe has observed, "In every aspect of the religious life, American faith has met American culture—and American culture has triumphed." Though perhaps worded a bit strongly, Wolfe's point is well taken. For Christians and Christianity to be the dominant religious demographic in our nation that it is, there is very little evidence of the salt that should be affecting our nation. One reason is clear: we have tried at least four approaches to cultural engagement—to retreat, to revive, to recapture and to reflect—and none of them have succeeded.

Retreat. The strategy of retreat is what marked much of American fundamentalism and still typifies the approach of many followers of Christ. A strategy of retreat involves pulling back from culture and creating a subculture of our own that acts like a protective bubble against the corrosive influence of the world around us. The idea is that culture is, by its very nature, an infectious disease. We must quarantine ourselves as much as possible in order to keep ourselves from sickness.

Some make this separation quite consciously; others exist in the bubble without knowing it—such as Christians who listen to Christian radio, watch Christian TV, patronize Christian bookstores, exercise in a Christian-themed aerobics class, socialize exclusively with Christian friends, home school their children in Christian co-ops and vacation at Christian retreats. They would not call themselves a classic fundamentalist in terms of a retreat from culture, and it is not that any of these pursuits are in and of themselves wrong, but taken together this represents an isolation from the world that constitutes a *functional* retreat.

There are, of course, more subtle examples of "retreat." Many who would say they hold retreat in contempt, giving as evidence their embrace of higher education and wide reading, are quick to denounce the use of all mediums of popular culture for their ministry. Yet popular culture is, by its very definition, the essence of culture. Consider the prominent theologian who so believes the "medium is the message," borrowing from the insights of communications theorist Marshall McLuhan, that he equates the move from a raised podium in the center of the church to a pulpit, and the pulpit to a Plexiglas stand, and then a Plexiglas stand to a barstool with a cup of Starbucks nearby, to the loss of the Word of God being central and "human connecting" becoming more important than hearing from God. Conclusion? Such "changes to our method" are really "changes in the message that is delivered." In other words, to protect and preserve the gospel from the culture, we must retreat from all things contemporary in culture. Of course, the irony is that even such missives as this are delivered through contemporary mediums of communication.

But is retreat always misguided? No. Cultural retreat arguably is the guiding principle of God's cultural directives to the people of Israel in the Old Testament. This separation was necessary for the initial creation and then subsequent preservation of their culture. From this we could contend that the more alien our surroundings become to the gospel, the more withdrawn we may have to become in order to preserve the distinctive nature of our own identity. But it is more accurate to say that as the distance between Christ and culture grows, the more clearly we need to draw the lines between being "in" the world but not "of" it. But make no mistake—we are to be *in it*. The Israelites were clearly led into a land full of alien ideas and sensibilities in order to dwell—and from that dwelling, to provide a bridge on to the human scene across which God's great redemptive drama could continue forward. Or consider Daniel and his role in the Babylonian world. His place in that deeply pagan culture was, to say the least, mainstream. His personal standards, however, were not. His retreat was not from culture itself but from culture's gods.

Revive. A second strategy is the quest to "revive" culture. The resolve to pray *for* and desire the experience *of* revival can be found throughout the biblical narrative. And few would deny the cultural impact such movements of God can bring.

Twice in North American history God has brought about national revivals. The first reached its peak in the colonies in the years 1740-1742. Often referred to as the Great Awakening, it was led by such luminaries as Jonathan Edwards and George Whitefield.

This was followed in the late-eighteenth and early-nineteenth centuries by the Second Great Awakening, which gave birth to the modern missionary movement. Specifically, the haystack prayer meeting of five collegians at Williams College in Massachusetts, given its name because the momentous night when the Holy Spirit blew through their lives, they were forced into a barn by a thunderstorm and found themselves praying under a

Figure 3.2. Methodist camp meeting, published by H. R. Robinson

haystack. From that group was Samuel Mills who became one of the founders of the American Bible Society; another member joined the first team of five missionaries to India. These revivals produced unprecedented mass evangelism, groundbreaking missionary activity and significant social change throughout North America.

I confess I am very attracted to this approach and have given a great deal of my life to pursuing it—but by itself, revival is insufficient. I was reminded of this when I spoke on the campus of Williams College at the invitation of the C. S. Lewis Foundation in honor of the two hundredth anniversary of the great haystack meeting. After I spoke in Thompson Memorial Chapel, built in 1905 to be the visible center for the school's spiritual life, a local pastor in attendance remarked how my address was the first time the gospel had been proclaimed there in his memory. In other words, the haystack awakening did not have a long-lasting influence. But more critically, a dependence on revival can lead to a passive approach to cultural engagement. I'm not suggesting that prayer is passive or that a revival—once unleashed—is by any means tame. But to simply wait for, hope for or look to revival to solve the challenge of cultural engagement is a passive approach, and we would be hard pressed to find any biblical support for such "waiting." As Leonard Ravenhill wrote,

> I am fully aware that there are those who in their sleepiness will swing back to the sovereignty of God and say, "When He moves, revival will come." That is only halftruth. Do you mean that the Lord is happy that eightythree people per minute die without Christ? Have you fallen for the idea that the Lord is more willing that *many* should perish?

Recapture. A third approach is perhaps the most familiar to Christians of our day: the conscious attempt to recapture the culture for Christ. Much of this is rooted in the idea that ours was once a Christian nation, and we should actively work to return our governing bodies and laws back to their original intent.

And even among those who do not espouse "recapture," often there is a deep sense of fulfilling a Christian destiny. America's chosenness and special blessing from God has been a constant theme throughout U.S. history, beginning with the Puritans and their desire that, in the words of John Winthrop in 1630, "wee shall be as a Citty upon a Hill." Historian Conrad Cherry observes,

> Throughout their history Americans have been possessed by an acute sense of divine election. They have fancied themselves a New Israel, a people chosen for the awesome responsibility of serving as a light to the nations. . . . It has long been . . . the essence of America's motivating mythology.

The vision of a Christian America was again popularized in the late 1970s by evangelical authors Peter Marshall and David Manuel in *The Light and the Glory*. Marshall and Manuel held that America was founded as a Christian nation and flourished under the benevolent hand of divine providence, arguing further that America's blessings will remain only as long as America is faithful to God as a nation. In 1989 a team of evangelical historians—Mark Noll, Nathan Hatch and George Marsden—attempted to lay this somewhat dubious thesis to rest, but it continues as a popular framework for viewing American history among American evangelicals.

The Moral Majority of the 1980s found its genesis in such sentiments, and accordingly formed a top-down strategy for cultural change. If we could only have Christians in the White House, Congress and the Supreme Court, or among other leadership elites, then morality would be enacted and faith would once again find the fertile soil needed to establish its footing in individual lives. The Moral Majority apparently won through the election of Ronald Reagan as president. And his subsequent Supreme Court appointments throughout the 1980s brought great anticipation for substantive change. Yet there has been little real change as a result. Even the prime target—the striking down of the Supreme Court decision *Roe v. Wade*, which legalized abortion—remains the law of the land to this day.

Figure 3.3. President Ronald Reagan and Jerry Falwell, 1984

Further, the culture wars of the 1980s and 1990s is now widely viewed as one of the more distasteful episodes in recent memory. Many younger evangelicals want nothing to do with what was often its caustic, abrasive and unloving approach toward those apart from Christ. So the effort to recapture the nation failed as a strategy and alienated a younger generation.

Reflect. One of the leading reactions to the "recapture" approach is perhaps most aptly termed a "reflect" strategy; like a mirror we reflect culture and its values. Rather than trying to take over culture, we embrace culture in the attempt to "become all things to all men so that by all possible means" we might save some (1 Corinthians 9:22). There can be little doubt that evangelical Christianity has been captive in a cultural ghetto of its own making. To break free of such bondage, many have made the effort to build bridges of understanding and relationship. Whether through the use of contemporary music or film, secular venues or vernacular, the goal has been to create a means for connecting with the culture. So rather than railing against pornography, some have set up booths at the AVN Adult Entertainment Expo in Las Vegas with the message "Jesus loves porn stars."

While laudable and often necessary, some efforts to reflect culture have slid into mere mirroring. Rather than working in and through culture in the form of Paul on Mars Hill, or creating a Mars Hill culture of dialogue and openness, there is a growing movement that seems to reflect the values of Mars Hill *itself* in order to gain a hearing; actually becoming the people we are attempting to reach and creating cultures that reflect our world rather than build bridges to reach it. Consider the recent blog post of one young Christian leader who, articulating his stance on homosexuality, felt himself

drifting toward acceptance that gay persons are fully human persons and should be afforded all of the cultural and ecclesial benefits that I am. . . .

I now believe that GLBTQ [Gay, Lesbian, Bisexual, Transgender and Queer] can live lives in accord with biblical Christianity (at least as much as any of us can!) and that their monogamy can and should be sanctioned and blessed by church and state.

Yes to being fully human persons; no to GLBTQ who embrace such lifestyles being blessed by the church. Such blessing is not reaching into a culture with the love of Christ; it is becoming that culture. The intent behind Paul's suggestion to "become all things" was never behavioral. We are not to so reflect the culture that its values and ideas are mirrored in our own values and beliefs. Paul's intent was to build bridges of understanding on which two parties could meet. It is one thing to reach out to porn stars; it is another to embrace pornography.

Much of this flows from our cultural insecurities. We want to be accepted by culture, not simply because we want a hearing, but because we long for cultural standing. In our efforts to distance ourselves from such enterprises as the Moral Majority, we seem fixated on fitting in—and being just as "hip" as the next person. We have seemed to succumb to what some have called the "celebrification" of culture—an awkward term, perhaps, but like "industrialization" and "bureaucratization," it speaks to a broad and historical trend: the increasing centrality of celebrities in our culture. Movie and television stars, professional athletes and musicians, and business moguls and journalists have captured our attention as never before. Joseph Epstein writes that "a received opinion about America in the early twenty-first century is that our culture values only two things:

money and celebrity." From this, celebrities have become our cultural commentators, charity spokespersons, role models and political candidates. They have become the arbiters of taste, morality and public opinion. Richard Schickel, who has written for *Time* magazine since 1972, reflects, "No issue or idea in our culture can gain any traction with the general population unless it has celebrity names attached to it."

As a result, there is a seduction to move from building bridges in and through such a celebrity culture to reach the world, to building bridges in and through celebrity culture in order to be *accepted* by the world. Or to become celebrities ourselves. Often the goal turns to getting to be an insider rather than on the outskirts of culture, leading some Christians to cling to Bono more than Bonhoeffer. As one tongue-in-cheek blogger, playing off the many motivational posters, phrased it, "Cultural Awareness: Following Bono to the Pub, to the Concert, and to the Uttermost Parts of the Earth."

Renewal. There is something to be said for all four of these strategies. The monastics' retreat from the world produced strength to serve others, keeping the medieval world from entering what truly would have been a dark age. While we are not to passively wait for revival, we are to labor in prayer and work for it to break out. And as much as we might be tempted in these days to demonize all attempts at recapturing our nation through the political realm, the Bible is replete with pivotal figures who did indeed change the course of human history through their active engagement of civic life—from Joseph to Nehemiah to Daniel and Esther. Finally, reflecting culture to build bridges over which two parties can meet lies at the heart of the Great Commission.

Yet all four seem lacking. They fall short of the ultimate goal. Instead of retreat, revival, recapture or reflection, I believe we should take the best of all four and aim for something deeper and more lasting.

Mark Galli, editor at *Christianity Today*, has written that our goal is not cultural transformation as much as it is personal obedience and service. As has often been noted, neither Jesus nor Paul seemed particularly concerned about addressing the immediate and most obvious (to the people of that day) cultural challenges of the Roman Empire. He did not seem as interested in altering that kingdom as much as ushering in an altogether new one, and he as much as told Pilate, when questioned, exactly that.

We are to be witnesses; we are to make disciples; we are to do justice, love mercy, feed the hungry, and care for the widow and orphan. This is far from pursuing a privatized faith; we are called to be present in culture as salt. Which, of course, can and often should lead to transformation—but more to the point, it can lead to renewal.

But what does renewal mean?

In *Culture Making*, Andy Crouch refers to it as the practice of "making" culture, drawing on the biblical ideas of creation and cultivation. Too often, he writes, we have settled for condemning, critiquing, copying or consuming culture. All have their place but pale in comparison to the deeper ideas of creation and cultivation. Sociologist James Davison Hunter argues similarly, maintaining that cultural transformation only occurs through cultural renewal, such as "compelling artistic and intellectual works produced by a movement of cultural visionaries and the networks they build." Once such visionaries gain a foothold in society, their words galvanize a culture. Our tools for such an effort have never changed: prayer, evangelism, example, argument, action and suffering.

But the dilemma is that we too often do not know what we

should make in our culture. We know to act, but where? We are willing to suffer, but for which cause? We are to embody faith, hope and love—but to what end? As T. S. Eliot noted,

> It is not enough simply to see the evil and injustice and suffering of this world, and precipitate oneself into action. What we must know, what only theology can tell us, is why these things are wrong. Otherwise, we may right some wrongs at the cost of creating new ones.

What is the cultural target on the wall? Yes, God's kingdom, but what does the reign of that kingdom entail? In terms of what actually constitutes kingdom culture, *truth*, *goodness* and *beauty* have been called the three fundamental values—the worth of anything can be exhaustively judged by reference to these three standards. Everything that *is* is related to whether it is true or false, good or evil, beautiful or ugly. Truth, goodness and beauty constitute what we are trying to achieve through our efforts to renew this culture as followers of Christ. But that simply begs the question: what is the true, the good and the beautiful?

Perhaps some pictures will help.

THE TRUE

During a recent trip to Washington, D.C., I met with a group of highly influential Christians involved in public policy, including lobbyists, lawyers in the Justice Department and presidential appointees. To a person, they had a clear sense of calling to their role, and they were frustrated that other followers of Christ were often critical about how they were pursuing that calling. To some, the only appropriate way to be a Christian in Washington is to share Christ on every elevator, make speeches littered with Scripture on the congressional floor and insist on biblical language in every policy. Instead, these Christians understand their calling is rooted in the dynamics of common grace, finding its most effective expression in the appeal to natural law.

Common grace is extended to all human beings through God's general providence (see Matthew 5:45; Hebrews 1:2-3; John 1:1-4). For example, consider the nurture of rain and sun, and the resulting bounty of a harvest. This is not to be confused with *prevenient* grace, meaning the specific grace that runs "before" (the meaning of the Latin *preveniens*) and enables a decision for Christ, affording individuals the ability to respond to God's call for salvation. Instead, common grace, wrote theologian Stanley Grenz, "speaks of God's extension of favor to all people through providential care, regardless of whether or not they acknowledge and love God."

And what has this to do with Christians in Washington and the creation of what is "true"? The Anglican scholar Philip Edgcumbe Hughes explains:

> Common grace is evident in the divine government or control of human society. It is true that human society is in a state of sinful fallenness. Were it not for the restraining hand of God, indeed, our world would long since have degenerated into a self-destructive chaos of iniquity, in which social order and community life would have been an impossibility.

Those who attempt to honor Christ within the Washington Beltway actively participate in and work for the extension of common grace. And we should be glad for such commitment. As Charles Colson writes,

> Understanding Christianity as a worldview is important not only for fulfilling the great commission but also for

fulfilling the cultural commission—the call to create a culture under the lordship of Christ. God cares not only about redeeming souls but also about restoring his creation. He calls us to be agents not only of his saving grace but also of his common grace. Our job is not only to build up the church but also to build a society to the glory of God.

On what basis do they pursue common grace? Most often through an appeal to natural law. The principles of natural law, such as the law of gravity, are found in nature itself. For Christians engaged in public policy, natural law provides the basis on which to appeal to conscience about good and evil. Through natural law Christians in a secular setting can appeal to what is right among those who do not believe that the Bible is a truth source. Yet natural law allows Christians to lead people *to* that truth source. The appeal to natural law provided the foundation for the moral philosophy of Thomas Aquinas, and with important modifications it was employed by Martin Luther and John Calvin. More recently, the arguments of C. S. Lewis in *Mere Christianity* made ample use of natural law.

So unlike Peter speaking to the God-fearing Jews in Jerusalem (Acts 2), those in Washington find a clearer model in Old Testament characters such as Joseph, Daniel and Esther. They worked within secular settings in obedience to God and affected those systems for God.

This is renewing culture toward the "true."

THE GOOD

For over fifty years Michael Haynes served as pastor of the historic Twelfth Baptist Church in the Roxbury district of downtown Boston. Twelfth Baptist Church is a direct descendant of the First African Baptist Meeting House on Beacon Hill, founded in 1805. In 1840, a band of dissenters from the church felt led of the Holy Spirit to become involved in the Underground Railroad, an organized means of smuggling slaves from bondage in the South to freedom in the North.

When I first met Michael, I asked him what he did. He said he was a pastor of a church. "Just a little church, in Roxbury. That's my ministry. Just three or four city blocks." One of the first persons on those blocks that he had a chance to serve was a young man named Martin Luther King Jr., who was given his first local church ministry opportunity by Michael.

Figure 3.4. Rev. Michael Haynes and Dr. Martin Luther King Jr.

Michael kept serving those few city blocks, always with a vision for changing them. And they needed change: Michael's has been a world of drug dealers, pimps, gangs, poverty, homelessness and racism. He knew from the beginning that any real change would rest on leadership. Not just his leadership but a generation of leaders. Leaders like Martin. But even more to the point, though he would never make such a claim, leaders like himself who would take up residence on their own few blocks in areas around the country and around the world where nobody would naturally want to reside. So he began talking about training leaders, praying about training leaders, casting vision about training leaders, until finally he witnessed its reality. First with a few classes at Twelfth Baptist, then as an extension center of a seminary, finally as a full-fledged urban campus.

Today you can travel to Roxbury and visit the Center for

Urban Ministry Education (CUME) campus. Today, CUME has become one of the leading urban training centers in the United States, teaching every week in six languages, developing hundreds of leaders for urban ministry. Fittingly it meets in the Michael E. Haynes building, one block down from Twelfth Baptist, one of Michael's "just three or four city blocks."

Three or four blocks of the "good."

THE BEAUTIFUL

Beauty relates to enjoyment and aesthetics, and of the great values it is perhaps the most overlooked. Yet in a truly decaying culture, it is often the first to lose its moorings. All the more reason to be alarmed by a recent social experiment staged by essayist Gene Weingarten and the *Washington Post* at 7:51 a.m. on Friday, January 12, 2007, in the middle of the morning rush hour at the L'Enfant Plaza Metro station in Washington, D.C. A nondescript, youngish white man in jeans, long-sleeved T-shirt and Washington Nationals baseball cap removed a violin from a small case. Placing the open case at his feet, he threw in a few dollars to seed the giving and began to play.

But this was no ordinary performer. The fiddler standing against the wall was thirty-nine-year-old Joshua Bell, one of the finest classical musicians in the world, playing some of the most elegant music ever written on a $3.5 million Stradivarius. During the next forty-three minutes, as the violinist performed six classical pieces, 1,097 people passed by. Would they have time for beauty? Would they even recognize it?

No.

Bell was almost entirely ignored. From over a thousand people, only six or seven even took notice.

This is deeper than a question of taste. One of the great breaks from the flow of the history of Western thought is our modern tendency to reduce the idea of beauty to a matter of subjective preference as opposed to an objective value, or even further, a glimpse of the divine. Consider David's great desire to "gaze upon the beauty of the LORD" (Psalm 27:4) or the declaration "From Zion, perfect in beauty, / God shines forth" (Psalm 50:2). This was not a subjective assessment—God *is* beauty; and true beauty, wherever it resides—along with the true and the good—is a glimpse of God himself.

And we need more glimpses.

- 4 -

OF TABERNACLES
AND MOSQUES

How Much Do You Have to
Hate Someone to Not Proselytize?

Keep this up much longer and you'll make a Christian out of me!

KING AGRIPPA TO THE APOSTLE PAUL

ACTS 26:28 *THE MESSAGE*

A recent front page of the *New York Times* contained an article titled "Old Church Becomes Mosque in Altered and Uneasy Britain," which told of a former Christian church in Clitheroe, England, that was to become a mosque. A second article on the same day, a bit more buried but still prominent in length, was titled "After Two Years of Work, an Updated Tabernacle," revealing how the Salt Lake Tabernacle, completed in 1867 by Mormon faithful and home to the famed Mormon Tabernacle Choir, was nearing the completion of its two-year renovation.

The two stories were actually one story—and a very important one.

Figure 4.1. Salt Lake Tabernacle, Utah

As a culture, we are rediscovering the validity of spiritual-ity, once again making room for insight, intuition and even revelation. Articles on angels, near-death experiences, prayer and healing have become cover stories. Spiritual themes run throughout contemporary music. Films and television increas-ingly explore religious ideas and settings. People are interested in spiritual things, they're asking spiritual questions and are beginning to see that many of their deepest needs are spiritual in nature.

But as the two stories in the *New York Times* demonstrate, this does not mean Christianity will benefit. In the new search for the spiritual, Christianity may lose while others gain. Or there may be such an eclectic gathering of spiritual commit-ments that Christianity will, at best, be only sampled. You may have heard of the term *metrosexual*. A metrosexual is a man found deep in the hair-care aisle or in the salon having his nails buffed to the perfect shine, while he's checking out the latest fashion magazines. He's a sensitive, well-educated urban dweller in touch with his feminine side. He loves to shop, wear jewelry and fill his bathroom counter with moisturizers—and maybe even makeup. In other words, he embodies a new definition of what it means to be a man. One that borrows heavily from what it means to be a woman, and combines it into a new identity.

Think of people becoming metrospirituals.

There is a keenly felt emptiness resulting from a secularized, materialistic world that has led to a hunger for something more, but many go no further than the search for an *experience*. We have come to the point where the soul cannot be denied, but all we know to do is search for something "soulish." So an extra-terrestrial will serve as well as an angel; a spiritualist as well as a minister. Borrowing a phrase from historian Christopher Dawson, we have a new form of secularism that embraces "religious emotion divorced from religious belief." In our current climate, people might be as likely to explore Wicca as the Word, Scientology as the Spirit.

Or they may, in the end, explore nothing at all.

A LAND OF SWEDES

When the 2008 American Religious Identification Survey (ARIS) was released, much was to be expected: mainlines are losing ground, the Bible belt is less Baptist, Catholics have infiltrated the South, denominationalism is on the wane. What was most alarming was the increase in "nones"—nearly doubling from 8 percent to 15 percent, making those who claim no religion at all the third largest defined constituency in the United States, eclipsed only by Catholics and Baptists. Further, "nones" were the only religious bloc to rise in percentage in every single state, thus constituting the only true national trend. As the ARIS report concludes, "the challenge to Christianity . . . does not come from other religions but from a rejection of all forms of organized religion." Barry Kosmin, co-researcher for the survey, warns against blaming secularism for driving up the percentage of Americans who say they have no religion. "These people aren't secularized. They're not thinking about religion and rejecting it; they're not thinking about it at all."

It is not that unbelief is driving out belief, James Turner suggests, but that unbelief has become more readily available as an answer to the question "What about God?" Unbelief is becoming mainstreamed, as evidenced by Barack Obama's recognition of people without faith, the first president to do so, in his inaugural address.

Thus, we must see America as a mission field. As an Episcopalian priest from South Carolina recently offered, "A couple came in to my office once with a yellow pad of their teenage son's questions. One of them was: 'What is that guy doing hanging up there on the plus sign?' " But America is not just any mission field—but a very specific one. As in "think Sweden." In his book *Society Without God*, sociologist Phil Zuckerman chronicled his fourteen months investigating Danes' and Swedes' religion. His conclusion? Religion "wasn't really so much a private, personal issue, but rather, a non-issue." His interviewees just didn't care about it. As one replied, "I really have never thought about that. . . . It's been fun to get these kinds of questions that I never, never think about." Sociologist Peter Berger once quipped, "If India is the most religious country on our planet, and Sweden is the least religious, America is a land of Indians ruled by Swedes." What we must now realize is that we are increasingly becoming a land of Swedes.

I would think such a climate would provide the perfect motivational setting for evangelism: spiritual openness, coupled with spiritual desire and hunger for spiritual experience, yet divorced from Christian belief. Yet this is not what is happening; the largest evangelical denominations, such as the Southern Baptist Convention, are not exhibiting a rise in baptisms but a steady, multiyear decline. And what about the mosque and the tabernacle? It would seem such stories will soon become commonplace. Muslims are likely to outnumber Christians in Britain in just a few decades, and the Mormon Church now claims twelve million members, including six million in the United States.

Why is it that this generation of Christians is losing such dramatic spiritual ground?

PASSIVITY

Most of us are familiar with the concept of urgency. It has to do with something that needs immediate attention because of its gravity. One of the challenges facing evangelical Christianity is that we do not seem to feel it is urgent to reach people for Christ. This despite an explicit effort from Jesus to generate such urgency:

> There was a rich man who was dressed in purple and fine linen and lived in luxury every day. At his gate was laid a beggar named Lazarus, covered with sores and longing to eat what fell from the rich man's table. Even the dogs came and licked his sores.
>
> The time came when the beggar died and the angels carried him to Abraham's side. The rich man also died and was buried. In hell, where he was in torment, he looked up and saw Abraham far away, with Lazarus by his side. So he called to him, "Father Abraham, have pity on me and send Lazarus to dip the tip of his finger in water and cool my tongue, because I am in agony in this fire."

But Abraham replied, "Son, remember that in your life-time you received your good things, while Lazarus received bad things, but now he is comforted here and you are in agony. And besides all this, between us and you a great chasm has been fixed, so that those who want to go from here to you cannot, nor can anyone cross over from there to us."

He answered, "Then I beg you, father, send Lazarus to my father's house, for I have five brothers. Let him warn them, so that they will not also come to this place of torment." (Luke 16:19-28)

When we die, we face either heaven or hell. While the great and final judgment was yet to come for both of these men, it's clear from this story that immediately upon our death, the fate of our lives is not only sealed but the verdict of that inevitable judgment is set in motion. The beggar Lazarus was by Abraham's side, which along with the concept of paradise, is mentioned in the Talmud as the home of the righteous—the place where the righteous dead go to await their future redemption and vindication. The rich man was in hell (Greek, "hades") the place where the wicked dead go to await their final judgment.

Figure 4.2. The parable of the rich man and Lazarus

And the chasm between the two cannot be crossed.

We do not often let our thoughts travel to such realities. It is uncomfortable. Even chilling. But one person in Jesus' story had it envelop every fiber of his being: the man in hell. To such a degree that he experienced a remarkable change in priorities. As I once heard someone observe, five minutes in hell made the rich man a flaming evangelist. Why? Because suddenly he knew it was all for real. And once he knew this, nothing mattered more than warning those he cared about. He knew that hell was not a figment of someone's imagination. It was real, and real people go there for eternity. And the man in hell knew that it would take someone going to them, talking to them, making it clear to them.

Hell has a way of making that evident.

We must realize that our friends, our family members, that person in our neighborhood, the person we work with who does not know Christ is in real trouble. We must not see the needs of the world solely in terms of food and clothing, justice and mercy, shelter and companionship. We must see those needs, to be sure, and meet them—but we must see beyond them to the fallen nature of a world and humanity that *produced* those needs. We must see eternity waiting to be written in their hearts. I know of a ministry to young male prostitutes working the streets of Chicago that offers food, shelter, counseling and an array of other social services to help men move out of that degrading lifestyle. Most of us would think that is more than enough, that the greatest issue had been addressed. But not John Green, the leader of Emmaus Ministries, who has said, "We do violence to the poor if we don't share Christ with them."

And he's right.

It is difficult to imagine passivity in regard to those who have yet to embrace the Christian faith. The Scriptures do not simply speak, they thunder:

We are therefore Christ's ambassadors, as though God were making his appeal through us. (2 Corinthians 5:20)

Go into all the world and preach the good news to all creation. (Mark 16:15)

Therefore go and make disciples of all nations, baptizing them in the name of the Father and of the Son and of the Holy Spirit, and teaching them to obey everything I have commanded you. (Matthew 28:19-20)

I have become all things to all men so that by all possible means I might save some. (1 Corinthians 9:22)

One Saturday night, just as we were beginning the first of our weekend services, a tragic car accident happened in front of our church's main entrance. A thirty-five-year-old man accidentally crossed the median line and ran into a car coming in the opposite direction. He wasn't wearing a seatbelt and was thrown from his car. He died on the scene. The "scene" being the side of the road by our front sign. Members and staff from our church were the first by his side. No one knew who he was.

It goes without saying that a death of any kind is unsettling. But a death in front of a church brings everything about our lives and mission into unique focus.

That night, as I drove from our campus, I could only think, *Was he a Christ follower? Did anyone ever reach out to him? What comfort is there in his family right now?* I was told there was a child's safety seat in the back of his truck. *Was he a father?* I could not shake the depth of that human tragedy—and the consequences. Not just in regard to the immediate throes of grief that would descend upon all who knew him, but the consequences of his death for eternity.

I took it upon myself to find out who he was. His name was

John. He was thirty-five years old. He had a young wife and a twenty-two-month-old daughter. I called the pastor of the church who was doing the funeral. It was a little Baptist church not far from our own. I learned that the entire church was in a state of shock, and that they took the following Sunday to try to process his death together, as a family of faith. Their one consolation? They knew he was a Christian. John was a Sunday school teacher and deeply committed to his faith. And while I was still aware of the enormous pain that surrounded his death, inside, I whispered a prayer of gratitude.

There were heroes around John's death that Saturday. Some of them were members of my church, along with medics, firefighters, police officers—all doing all that they could to save a life. And it was so clear what needed to be done. It was so obviously urgent. But in truth, the real saving had already been done, because another group of people saw the urgency surrounding his life in another way. The real heroes were the people who saved John before he died. And the best response of our church was not to run up the hill to serve at the scene of an accident, but to reach out to the thousands who drive by our campus in their cars every day. For each one will, in their own way and time, meet an equally fateful end.

Yet it is precisely this challenge that seems to have fallen on deaf ears. According to the International Programs Center, U.S. Bureau of the Census, at the time of this writing, the total population of the world is 6,793,790,293. Over two billion of them are Christians. That's one out of every three persons on the planet. But according to the latest research from Todd M. Johnson, research fellow and director of the Center for the Study of Global Christianity, most non-Christians have never met a follower of Christ. Over 86 percent of all Buddhists, Hindus and Muslims do not even *know* a Christian. Globally, over 80 percent of all non-Christians do not personally know a Christian. It would seem that we have confused the command to not be *of* the world with not being *in* it—particularly in terms of relationships with those who do not share our faith. We are isolated from the very people we say we long to reach, having seemingly retreated into a subculture of our own making.

This was not the model of Jesus.

He went into the world; he spent time with those who were far apart from God. He reached out relationally, built friendships, went into their homes, attended their parties, broke bread at their tables. It was profoundly intentional and openly risqué, to such a degree that he was derisively called a friend of sinners.

The scandal of Jesus' interaction with the unchurched is often lost on modern readers of the Gospels. So he went to a party of Matthew's? So he ate with Zacchaeus? So he spoke to a woman at a well? He was just being courteous, akin to someone who would open the door for a young mother or help an elderly person across the street. Such matters are passed over quickly to get to the heart of the story. But attending Matthew's party, eating with Zacchaeus and speaking to the woman *is* the story. In the ancient world "table fellowship" was considered an act of intimacy—arguably among the closest of intimacies. This helps explain the depth of betrayal David felt when he spoke of those with whom he had shared bread but who then turned against him (Psalm 41), as well as the pain Jesus felt when Judas—immediately after taking the bread from his hand—went out into the night for his thirty pieces of silver.

To eat with someone, particularly a "sinner," was far more than a meal. It signified welcome, recognition and acceptance. Eating with sinners simply was not to be done—not even in the name of redemption: "Let not a man associate with the wicked, even to bring him near to the law," went the later rabbinic saying. This is why we read of the shock and dismay that Jesus was virtually indiscriminate with whom he ate (Luke 14—15). But he was more than just willing to meet and speak with those far from God. He was passionately intentional, proclaiming that such interactions rested at the heart of his mission:

> Who needs a doctor: the healthy or the sick? I'm here inviting outsiders, not insiders—an invitation to a changed life, changed inside and out. (Luke 5:31-32 *The Message*)

> [I] came to seek and to save what was lost. (Luke 19:10)

> Go out to the roads and country lanes, and urge the people there to come so my house will be full. (Luke 14:23 NCV)

At the time of this writing, Mecklenburg Community Church has just over 79 percent of its total growth coming from the unchurched. Leaders from other churches often ask what we do to reach such large numbers of non-Christians. They want a program, a style, a series, anything that might translate to their context and work. The reality is that our strategy is constantly changing; our "secret," however, has remained the same for nearly two decades: we are committed to reaching out in the most effective way possible. It's that simple. We do not believe we exist for ourselves but for those who have yet to come. We do not build the church to meet our needs but the needs of others. Our "front door" has been intentionally, passionately, thrown open, and we do not simply invite others in but actively seek them out and bring them.

In explaining this to others, I often tell of an event that happened in the early days of Meck. We spent four years meeting in an elementary school, which meant we had to set up every Saturday and break down every Sunday. One weekend we were breaking down after the service, putting things back in trucks and sheds and cars, and Susan and I looked around and realized that our daughter, Rebecca, wasn't there. I thought she was with Susan, and Susan thought she was with me. She was only about seven years old at the time. At first, we only panicked a little, because we assumed she'd be found right around the corner.

But she wasn't right around the corner.

She wasn't out on the playground, she wasn't in any of the rooms, she wasn't in the hallway, she wasn't in the cafeteria, and she wasn't in the gym. We couldn't find her anywhere. I have seldom experienced such sheer panic and fear.

My little girl, *gone*.

I started racing through the building, going into rooms we didn't even use, hallways that were darkened, I ran outside and yelled her name until I thought I was going to lose my voice. Nothing mattered more to me than finding my daughter. It occupied every thought, every ounce of energy. Everything else paled in comparison.

Just as we were getting ready to call the police, going back over every inch of the school again, I saw, down a long, dark hallway that we didn't use, outside of the doors we always blocked off because it was so cut off and led directly to the fields, a little head with brown hair barely above the glass. She had gone out the door, it had locked behind her, so she had sat down where she couldn't be seen and was just waiting for someone to find her. She had been crying and was scared, and she didn't know what to do but wait.

I ran down that hallway, threw open those doors and grabbed that little girl and held her like you would not believe. You could not have pried her from my arms.

That is the heart of God.

The heart of the Father is one in absolute, ongoing, permanent frenzy to find the lost. And that is to be our frenzy as well.

HOSTILITY

But there is more than just passivity that we must address. Many Christians view those outside of the faith as needing to go to hell. They are the bad guys, the enemy; we refer to them as "pagans," "secular humanists," "liberals" and worse. Our relationship seems intensely adversarial in nature. It's the pro-family, Christian-radio listening, fish-sticker wearing, big-Bible carrying types versus the left-leaning, evolution-believing, gay-marriage supporting, Harry Potter–reading pagans. And those outside of the faith have little doubt about our sentiments.

In their book *unChristian*, David Kinnaman and Gabe Lyons detail research on how those between the ages of sixteen and twenty-nine who are outside of the church view the church and people in it. They offered a set of words or phrases as possible descriptors of Christianity, and then cataloged the number who affirmed their accuracy. Leading the way was "antihomosexual" (91 percent) and "judgmental" (87 percent). "Outsiders believe Christians do not like them because of what they do, how they look, or what they believe," write Kinnaman and Lyons. "They feel minimized—or worse, demonized—by those who love Jesus."

Consider what has been our political voice—or at least, what has been perceived to be our voice. An editorial in *Christianity Today* titled "Hating Hillary" chronicled the depth of rancor and animosity among Christians toward Hillary Clinton, particularly during her run for the presidency. While her political stances have been polarizing, instead of civil discourse there was an avalanche of animosity expressed in everything from T-shirts, bumper stickers, voodoo dolls and "No Way In Hellary" barbecue aprons. At the 2004 Republican convention, a spokesman for the Family Research Council passed out fortune cookies with the message: "#1 reason to ban human cloning:

Hillary Clinton." In anticipation of her historic run, which would have made her the first female president in U.S. history, the late Jerry Falwell announced at a 2006 Values Voter Summit, "I certainly hope that Hillary is the candidate. Because nothing would energize my [constituency] like Hillary Clinton. If Lucifer ran, he wouldn't."

So much for the "aroma of Christ" (2 Corinthians 2:15).

And it is easy to smell.

It reminds me of a story told by Martin Niemoller, a German Lutheran bishop who was called on to negotiate with Adolf Hitler during World War II in the attempt to save the church of Germany from being closed down by the Nazi dictator. Toward the end of his life Niemoller had a recurring dream in which he saw Hitler standing before Jesus on Judgment Day. Jesus got off his throne, put his arm around Hitler and asked, "Adolf! Why did you do the ugly, evil things you did? Why were you so cruel?" Hitler, with his head bent low, simply answered, "Because nobody ever told me how much You loved me." At this point, Niemoller would wake up from his dream in a cold sweat, remembering the countless meetings he had with Hitler—face to face—and he never once said, "By the way, Führer, Jesus loves you! He loves you more than you'll ever know. He loved you so much that He died for you. Do you know that?"

For Niemoller, this was a nightmare. For us, it is the heart of our challenge.

THE END FOR THE MEANS

But even among those who are neither passive nor hostile, the evangelistic mandate can still be muted if not silenced—largely through such an emphasis on connecting with the non-Christian that there is little vision for the relationship beyond the connection. It is as if the emphasis is on the temporal, not the eternal, in terms of focus and intent.

I spoke at the inaugural gathering of an annual event, simply titled "Q," that brings together the leading figures among emerging generations, all considered on the cutting edge of infiltrating and shaping culture for Christ. I have great respect for this event, its intent and its founders, and what follows is not meant to disparage "Q" in any way.

But it was an interesting visit.

I had arrived early enough to listen to preceding addresses and to capture some of the hallway conversations. There was much talk of reaching culture, impacting culture, shaping culture—and then it hit me. No one was talking about reaching the people who were making that culture. There was talk of justice and art, but not redemption. In some quarters it is as if we are focusing on the means to the end, only to forget the end. I have noticed this with many new churches planted to "reach the world" and "connect with culture." After sitting through countless such services, the pattern seems the same: enormous effort to connect culturally, great explanations of the practical wisdom and ethic of the Bible, but seldom is given the invitation to actually cross the line of faith in Christ.

When my turn came to speak, I went off script. I didn't plan on it—it was just one of those moments where as I was speaking the Holy Spirit planted a thought in my mind that I followed. I made a passing comment that we must not forget the most critical cultural engagement of all remains personal evangelism. In fact, I quipped that in many of the more advanced and "hip" conversations about cultural engagement, evangelism was conspicuous by its absence. I wasn't sure it was what I needed to say, but then I was besieged by large numbers afterward who seemed to be quite taken—if not shaken—by my offhand remark.

It seemed to be an important reminder.

I sense among some that the primary goal is to "get" culture and participate with it to be seen as current. But once we find ourselves in positions of cultural influence, or having created needed cultural bridges, then what? Historically, the most transformational of cultural revolutionaries did not merely understand or penetrate culture—they sought to redeem those in it. And wisely so. As Aleksandr Solzhenitsyn observed, "The line separating good and evil passes not through states, nor between classes, nor between political parties either, but right through every human heart. . . . It is impossible to expel evil from the world in its entirety, but it is possible to constrict it within each person."

The irony of our day is that never before has a generation of Christians—particularly young Christian leaders—cared more about connecting with their culture for the sake of Christ. The dilemma is that many are connecting, but once the connection is made, the gospel itself seems lost in translation. Or perhaps more accurately, lost in *transmission*. We must never forget that we relate to culture for a reason—its redemption. Many of us have lamented the loss of a whole gospel—meaning its reduction to nothing more than salvation for the world to come, overlooking the need to reach out to the poor and homeless, the AIDS infected and the victim of injustice. How tragic if we went from one half of the gospel to another half and never seized its whole transforming, revolutionary intent for the whole world.

THE GIFT OF A BIBLE

Now some might think, *But what if I turn them off? What if they react negatively?* This seems to be the arresting fear of our day. Those actually engaged in the effort are among the first to witness to its spurious assumptions. Most people—even the most hardened of skeptics—respond positively to a winsome and compelling witness.

Penn Jillette is the talkative half of Penn and Teller, the Las Vegas comedy-illusion team, now with their own program on Showtime titled *Penn and Teller: Bulls***!* Penn is an outspoken atheist. But he posted a video blog on his personal website about a man who gave him a Bible, which has much to teach Christians:

Figure 4.3. Penn Jillette

At the end of the show . . . we go out and we talk to folks, . . . sign an occasional autograph and shake hands. . . . [T]here was one guy waiting over to the side . . . [a]nd he walked over to me and he said, "I was here last night at the show, and I saw the show and I liked the show. . . ." He was very complimentary. . . .

And then he said, "I brought this for you," and he handed me a Gideon pocket edition. I thought it said from the New Testament. . . . And he said, "I wrote in the front of it, and I wanted you to have this. I'm kind of proselytizing." And then he said, "I'm a business man. I'm sane. I'm not crazy." And he looked me right in the eye and did all of this. And it was really wonderful.

I believe he knew that I was an atheist. But he was not defensive. . . . He was really kind and nice and sane and looked me in the eyes and talked to me, and then gave me this Bible. And I've always said that I don't respect people who don't proselytize. I don't respect that at all. If you believe that there is a heaven and hell and that people could be going to hell . . . How much do you have to hate somebody to not proselytize? How much do you have to hate somebody to believe that everlasting life is possible and not tell them that?

And that's all I want to say.

Perhaps, that's all we need to hear.

- 5 -

THE MARK OF A CHRISTIAN

BITTER BLOGS AND CIVILITY

I like your Christ, I do not like your Christians.
Your Christians are so unlike your Christ.

MOHANDAS GANDHI

The CNN program *Crossfire*, which boasted being about "left versus right, black versus white, paper versus plastic, the Red Sox against the Yankees," daringly invited comedian Jon Stewart on to the show after Stewart criticized them for their acerbic banter. Each week, two guests espousing opposing views were brought on the show to duke it out, and Stewart had noted the toxic fumes. Hoping, no doubt, for more sparks to fly, the guests were disarmed by Stewart with words they did not expect:

"Why do we have to fight?"

It is a good question. So good that shortly thereafter the show was cancelled due to declining ratings.

So why *do* we have to fight?

Sociologist Deborah Tannen writes that we live in an "argument culture." She observes that we no longer dialogue with each other; there has been a system-wide relational breakdown in our culture. It is as if we approach everything with a warlike mentality, so we end up looking at the world—and people—with an adversarial frame of mind.

How do we explore an idea? A debate.

How do we cover the news? Find people who express the most extreme, polarizing views and present them as the "two sides."

Figure 5.1. John Stewart at the USO Merit Awards

How do we settle a dispute? Through litigation that pits one party against the other.

How do we begin an essay? Oppose someone, because criticizing and attacking reveals that we are really thinking.

The lack of civility in our world has become so pandemic that it is now widely chronicled by mainstream media as a cultural phenomenon. Consider a recent *USA Today* article "Rudeness, Threats Make the Web a Cruel World," or a *New York Times* article on Wikipedia's "impolite" side. In his book *A Bee in the Mouth*, Peter Wood speaks of this in terms of "anger in America." Sadly, this seems to mark the very people who should be most immune to such animus.

Christians.

BROTHERS IN ARMS

A recent editorial in *Christianity Today* discussed how no attribute of civilized life seems more under attack than civility.

The author, David Aikman, noted the extent to which certain Christians have turned themselves into the

> self-appointed attack dogs of Christendom. They seem determined to savage not only opponents of Christianity, but also fellow believers of whose doctrinal positions they disapprove.
>
> A troll through the Internet reveals websites so drenched in sarcasm and animosity that an agnostic, or a follower of another faith tradition interested in what it means to become a Christian, might be permanently disillusioned.

I read of a large church that made the news due to a problem with a persistently caustic blogger. A former member, he had become disgruntled over various actions of the senior pastor, and became further incensed that the pastor maintained the backing of the church leadership. With nowhere to go with his animus, and no means to lobby for his cause, he started an anonymous blog in order to wage a one-person campaign of bitterness. It quickly disintegrated on both sides to such a degree that the church complained to the police, who investigated and discovered the identity of the blogger. Now suits and counter-suits are flying freely.

What a Godforsaken mess.

The article had Web links, which led to other links, and before I knew it, I found myself exposed in a way I had never imagined possible to the sordid world of the bitter blog, meaning blogs that exist for no other reason than to attack a particular Christian leader, church or ministry. I found that there is a bitter blog against virtually every senior pastor of a megachurch. Their purpose? Causing dissension and disunity and as much disaffection as possible.

When I started Mecklenburg Community Church, I commissioned a survey through the Barna Research Group to ask un-churched people who lived in the surrounding community a simple question: "Why don't you go to church?" The leading answers fell into categories you might expect: "There is no value in attending," "I don't have the time," "I'm simply not interested," "Churches ask for money too much," "Church services are usu-ally boring." What surprised me most was the second-most common answer for being unchurched, representing six out of every ten people: "Churches have too many problems."

The assessment of the unchurched is that the typical Chris-tian community is inflexible, hypocritical, judgmental and just plain mean. Division and discord are perceived to be more pres-ent in church than in many other groups. Why would anyone want to become involved with something that, in their mind, is so obviously dysfunctional? As one man in the survey quipped, "I've got enough problems in my life. Why would I go to church and get more?"

Sadly, this is not new for evangelicalism. I once read of a school president who was also an evangelist, who made it clear that if any faculty or student attended a certain fellow evangel-ist's crusade, they would be fired or expelled. If they wanted to pray for the evangelist, he suggested the following words:

> Dear Lord, bless the man who leads Christian people into disobeying the word of God, who prepares the way for Antichrist by building the apostate church and turning his so-called converts over to infidels and unbelieving preachers. Bless the man who flatters the Pope and defers to the purple and scarlet-clothed Antichrist who heads the church that the word of God describes as the old whore of Babylon.

So much for Bob Jones Sr. and his relationship with Billy

Graham. I am sure Bob Jones Sr. was a good and godly man in many ways. Just not in this way. But while this sentiment has been brewing for some time, what is new is the increasingly public nature of our vitriol, its widespread dissemination through the Internet and our growing comfort with its presence. As Francis Schaeffer observed toward the end of his life, it has almost become a matter of personal privilege: "We rush in, being very, very pleased, it would seem at times, to find other men's mistakes. We build ourselves up by tearing other men down, . . . we love the smell of blood, the smell of the arena, the smell of the bullfight."

We may be pleased, but we are not being Christian.

THE MARK OF A CHRISTIAN

In the Gospel of John we have the poignant final words and prayers of Jesus to his disciples before he went to the cross. Between John 13 and John 17, Jesus pours out his heart. This is considered by many to be among the most moving sections of the New Testament. What occupied Jesus the moments before his atoning death for the sins of the world? Not surprisingly, that the world would recognize his gift to them. How would that happen? Christ's torrent of prayer and pleading begins and ends with a passionate call for unity among those who claim his name. The observable love between those who called themselves his followers was *everything*. Why? Jesus said this unity, and this unity alone, would arrest the world's attention and confirm that he was from the Father.

We often marvel at the growth of the early church, the explosion of faith in Christ in such numbers and speed that in only a blink the Roman Empire had officially turned from paganism to Christianity. We look for reasons in formulas and programs, services and processes. The simple truth is that they

answered Jesus' prayer. Yes, as Michael Green has noted, they
shared the gospel like it was gossip over the backyard fence. But
what did people find when they responded to the evangelical
call? As Tertullian noted, the pagan reaction to the Christian
communal life was, "See how they love one another."

As has often been pointed out, when the Bible talks about
such loving unity, it doesn't mean uniformity, that is, everyone
looking and thinking alike. And
the biblical idea is certainly not
to be confused with unanimity,
that is, complete agreement about
every petty issue (though there
should be unity of purpose and
agreement on the major issues related to doctrine and mission). By
unity, the Bible means first and
foremost a oneness of heart—a
relational unity. Being kind to one
another, gracious to one another,
forgiving of one another, not as-
suming the worst, shooting the
wounded or being overly suspi-
cious. Biblical unity works through conflicts, avoids slander
and gossip, and is generous in spirit.

**Figure 5.2. The wine and
bread of Communion**

Unity matters—so much so that the Bible reserves some of
its harshest words of discipline for those who sin against it:
"Warn a divisive person once, and then warn him a second
time. After that, have nothing to do with him," wrote the apostle Paul (Titus 3:10). And in one of the most overlooked—or
more honestly, willfully ignored—passages of Scripture, Paul
also warned strongly against taking the Lord's Supper if we
have unresolved relational conflict in our life. So strongly is

God's feeling on this that it could—and indeed has—resulted in death.

It shouldn't surprise us. As we take of the body of Christ, we are to *be* the body of Christ. Paul writes:

> Is not the cup of thanksgiving for which we give thanks a participation in the blood of Christ? And is not the bread that we break a participation in the body of Christ? Because there is one loaf, we, who are many, are one body, for we all partake of the one loaf. (1 Corinthians 10:16-17)

The symbolic act of sharing from one loaf symbolizes the unity of the body of Christ, the church, which has as its source of nourishment the bread of life. The word *companion* is from two Latin words, *com*, which means "with," and *panis*, which means "bread." So the word *companion* literally means "with bread" or "breadfellow." We are companions because through the bread we are brought together; this is the body of Christ. From this comes Paul's charge:

> In the following directives I have no praise for you, for your meetings do more harm than good. In the first place, I hear that when you come together as a church, there are divisions among you. . . . When you come together [in this way], it is not the Lord's Supper you eat. (1 Corinthians 11:17-18, 20)

Paul is horrified that there isn't a sense of community at Communion. To be divided, or to despise another who shares bread with you, was nothing less than an abuse and even contradiction of the sacrament. If someone is at war with the body or is involved in division of the body, he or she should not take and eat of the body. Thus, Paul's reminder that some have gotten sick, even died, as discipline from the Lord because of the functional disavowal of Christian unity.

That's how serious unity in the church is to God. Because unity and love, as Francis Schaeffer pointed out, is *the* "mark" of the Christian. Not just a feeling of love or an acknowledgment of love, but a *demonstration* of love. And it is decisive not only to our faith but also to our witness. As Schaeffer writes:

> Jesus is giving a right to the world. Upon his authority he gives the world the right to judge whether you and I are born-again Christians on the basis of our observable love toward all Christians.
>
> That's pretty frightening. Jesus turns to the world and says, "I've something to say to you. On the basis of my authority, I give you a right: you may judge whether or not an individual is a Christian on the basis of the love he shows to all Christians."

It should be deeply convicting that the secular marketplace understands the importance of this more than many Christians. People expect great performance from products, services and experiences. So what makes some brands inspiring while others languish? Saatchi and Saatchi, a leading marketing firm, coined the term *Lovemarks* to reveal the answer, calling it the "future beyond brands." A Lovemark delivers beyond expectations, and thereby receives high levels of respect. They "reach your heart as well as your mind, creating an intimate, emotional connection that you just can't live without." Take a brand away and people will find a replacement. "Take a Lovemark away and people will protest its absence. You don't just buy Lovemarks, you embrace them passionately." You experience it.

Christianity is meant to be the ultimate Lovemark, and in light of our mission to the world it must be. Schaeffer was right when he maintained that the world cares little for doctrine.

Only one thing, Schaeffer maintained, will arrest the attention of a world that has disavowed the idea of truth: "The love that true Christians show for each other and not just for their own party." This is, Schaeffer concluded, the final apologetic. Unloving attitudes and words cause a "stench that the world can smell. . . . Our sharp tongues, the lack of love between us, . . . these are what properly trouble the world."

The dilemma is that the lack of love does not always seem to trouble us, and usually for two reasons. First, we simply do not see it as sin. It has become so commonplace, we no longer blush. I recall talking to the president of a leading Christian seminary. He said that soon after his appointment, when he went to his first faculty meeting as president, he couldn't believe the way the professors were talking to each other and the spirit that was being portrayed. The dialogue was negative, nasty, biting, vitriolic and unloving. Afterward, someone said to him, "Don't worry—that was normal—it's just the way we talk around here."

He couldn't help himself. "Well," he said, "it sure sounded like sin to me!"

He is right. It *was* sin.

I had a similar set of conversations at the start of my first pastorate. "That's just the way deacons' meetings are," "That's just the way business meetings go," "That's just the way he is."

The *acceptance* of lovelessness isn't what leads to its continued presence, but our justification of it. Specifically, the warped theology that feels loving actions and attitudes are only warranted when we have nothing provoking us! It is as if disagreement, disapproval and disenchantment sanction bad behavior. The bitter blog is justified *because;* the slanderous attack is warranted *because;* the angry accusation can be made *because.* It is an arresting theology, like driving past an accident on the side of the road is arresting—it is so sick, so sordid, so sad, it's difficult to take your eyes away from it. So the blogs get read, the flames get fanned, and the damage gets done.

But make no mistake.

It doesn't just sound like sin.

It *is* sin.

SECOND-DEGREE MURDER

There are two principal categories of sin—those of the flesh and those of the spirit. We have tended to pinpoint the glutton, drunkard and adulterer far more quickly than we have the prideful, arrogant, divisive, slanderous and mean-spirited. Even more, we have turned a blind eye to—if not celebrated—caustic, mean-spirited words, actions and attitudes as if they are not reprehensible.

In truth, these are second-degree murder.

In the Sermon on the Mount, Jesus said:

> You're familiar with the command . . . "Do not murder." I'm telling you that anyone who is so much as angry with a brother or sister is guilty of murder. Carelessly call a brother "idiot!" and you must might find yourself hauled into court. Thoughtlessly yell "stupid!" at a sister and you are on the brink of hellfire. The simple moral fact is that words kill. (Matthew 5:21-22 *The Message*)

I find Jesus' words very uncomfortable. I am more at ease with the musing of a Louisiana minister: "I don't hate anybody. 'Cause the Bible says it's a sin to hate. But there are some folks I hope dies of cancer of the tonsils." Yet Jesus reminds me that my biting words, my character assassinations, my slander, innuendo, gossip and snide remarks are every bit as hateful to the heart of God as the knife dripping with blood or a smoking gun. When we go on the warpath against others, becoming active in ruining their reputations, spreading accusations, uncharitably criticizing their behavior or taking verbal shots, we are emptying the contents of a gun in their direction. It's an assault with the intent to kill. The Bible is very clear on this:

> A word out of your mouth may seem of no account, but it can accomplish nearly anything—or destroy it! . . .
>   By our speech we can . . . throw mud on a reputation. . . . This is scary. . . . The tongue runs wild, a wanton killer. . . . With our tongues we . . . curse the very men and women [God] made in his image. . . .
>   My friends, this can't go on. (James 3:5-10 *The Message*)

The villagers of the Solomon Islands practice a unique form of logging. If a tree is too large to be felled with an ax, the natives cut it down by yelling at it. Woodsmen credited with special powers creep up on a tree at dawn and then scream at the tree at the top of their lungs. They continue this for thirty days. The tree, it is told, then dies and falls over. The villagers base their practice on the belief that hollering kills the spirit of the tree. According to the villagers, it always works. I don't know if their practice works on trees. I do know that it works on people.

THE DEADLY SIN OF ENVY

Why do we talk this way? What is keeping us from seeing this sin as sin? Because we do not acknowledge the root of the sin itself, which usually is not anger but envy. When we think of loveless behavior or broken community, we often assume anger is behind it. Anger is real, and in many cases it leads to this very sin. But Scripture tells us that divisions among us are often caused by envy, what Herman Melville called "the rabies of the heart." But we do not often diagnose this disease because envy is seldom explored. All the more reason why the evil one frequently uses it to incite division and discord. So what then is envy?

Envy arises when we want something desirable that belongs to another person. It could be physical appearance, a job, money, talent, position, a spouse, even children. As a result, envy is a vice of proximity—the closer someone is to us in terms of vocation, temperament, gifts or position, the more fertile is the soil in which envy grows. In the classic pattern, notes theologian Cornelius Plantinga, the prosperous envier resents the rich, the 3:58 miler resents the 3:54 miler, the pretty resent the beautiful, and the hardworking B+ student resents the A student, especially the happy-go-lucky one who never seems to study. Drawing from this aspect of envy in his fictitious portrayal of hell, Dante doomed the envious to having their eyes eternally sewn shut. Throughout their lives they used their vision to focus on others. Now their eyes were forever closed in punishment.

Yet envy doesn't stop at wanting the possessions of another person. It goes on to breed dislike, even hatred, toward the possessor of what we desire. This is captured in the word itself, which is drawn from the Latin *invidia*, which means "to look maliciously upon." The Greek term, as used in the New Testament, literally refers to having an "evil eye." Few have captured the dynamic of envy better than Irish writer Oscar Wilde, who told a fictional tale about the devil crossing the Libyan desert. He came upon a small number of demons who were tormenting a holy hermit. The saintly man easily shook off their evil suggestions. The devil stepped forward to give his lieutenants a lesson.

"What you do is too crude," he said. "Permit me for one moment."

He then whispered to the holy man, "Your brother has just been made Bishop of Alexandria." Suddenly, a look of malignant envy clouded the once-serene face of the hermit. Then the devil turned to his imps and said, "That is the sort of thing which I should recommend."

Most lovelessness flows from some form of envy. Even when not apparent, we often harbor a secret satisfaction at the misfortune of others: the business leader who is handcuffed and led from his office for fraud, the politician who is exposed for spinning a web of lies, the priest or pastor caught in adultery. The Germans have a word for it: *schadenfreude*, which means finding joy in the suffering of another. In the famed case of Cain and Abel, where Cain's offering to God was less esteemed than that of his brother's, only murder itself would satisfy Cain's wounded ego. This is why the Bible warns us of the sin of envy in such strong language: "If you harbor bitter envy and selfish ambition in your hearts, do not boast about it or deny the truth. Such 'wisdom' does not come down from heaven but is earthly, unspiritual, of the devil. For where you have envy and selfish ambition, there you find disorder and every evil practice" (James 3:14-16).

The antidote to envy is security, the kind of security that allows us to rejoice in the strengths of others while realizing our own uniqueness in Christ. In heaven, we won't be looking around to see what others have or how they have been rewarded by God. Instead, we'll be filled with awe and wonder at the gift Giver and his wonderful providence. The great prayer against envy, and hence the prayer toward love, is found in Psalm 73, which begins:

> When I was beleaguered and bitter,
>   totally consumed by envy,
> I was totally ignorant. (Psalm 73:21-22 *The Message*)

This is the confession we need to make. Not simply of the state of envy, but that it is rooted in ignorance of who we are, of who others are, and of the wisdom and will of God. It acknowledges the failure of envy to see life beyond these temporal shores and past our momentary wants and desires. The deeper truth that holds the antidote to envy is knowledge of the love of God and recognizing our own hand-fashioned nature.

> But you've taken my hand.
> You wisely and tenderly lead me,
> > and then you bless me. (Psalm 73:23-24 *The Message*)

The prayer then moves on to reflect how God is not simply active in the life of others but in our own lives as well. The words remind us of a plan that God is unfolding in our lives, and that his plan for us is a source of immeasurable blessing and security. Throughout our lives God is developing us, giving to us and using us in ways that are unique to who we are. Our security lies in the distinctive nature of our relationship with God and our trust that he knows best how to accomplish his plans. Ultimately it matters not where we are led or how we are used, but *that* we are led by God and that we participate with others in the grand scheme of his design.

> You're all I want in heaven!
> > You're all I want on earth! . . .
> I'm in the very presence of God—
> > oh, how refreshing it is! (Psalm 73:25, 28 *The Message*)

Then comes the affirmation that real fulfillment can be found in God alone. He replaces our envy with a desire for what he wants to bring into our life. We no longer desire what others have, but what God has for us! Even more important, our heart supremely calls for God himself. Rather than seeking the things possessed by others, we seek a Person, the source of our security.

AMAZING GRACE

But assaulting envy's hold is not enough to unleash love and cement the mark of Christ in our lives. We need Christ and his work. We have seen that love is the mark of the Christian, but the world too loves. What kind of love, then, are we to pursue?

There was a British conference on comparative religions that brought together experts from all over the world to debate what was unique, if anything, about the Christian faith. Was it the idea that a god became a man? No, other religions had variations on that. Even the great Greek myths were about gods appearing in human form. Was it the resurrection? No. The idea of the dead returning to life could be found in many different ideologies. Was it heaven, life after death or an eternal soul? Was it love for your neighbor, good works, care for the poor or homeless? Was it sin or hell or judgment?

The debate went on for some time, until the famous author C. S. Lewis wandered into the room. Lewis had journeyed from atheism to agnosticism, evaluating the many differences between the various world religions and coming to Christianity in the end. Lewis asked what all of the debate was about, and discovered that his colleagues were trying to identify Christianity's unique contribution among world religions.

"Oh, that's easy," said Lewis. "It's grace."

And after they thought about it, they had to agree.

At its heart grace is getting what we don't deserve, and not getting what we do. It's something we receive that we do not deserve. The idea of God's love coming to us free of charge, without strings attached, seems to go against every instinct within the human race. The Buddhist Eightfold Path, the Hindu doctrine of karma, the Jewish covenant, Muslim obedience—they're all ways of trying to earn approval. Only Christianity contends that God's love is unconditional.

This is not only the distinguishing love mark of the Christian, but it is what compels our love for each other. Our love for one another is based on the realization that *our* relationship with Christ is built on grace, and therefore our relationship with others should be as well. To love others is to consider them as Christ has considered us, which is through the eyes of grace. Therefore we are to extend that grace to each other. When we don't, we become like the ungrateful servant that Jesus once spoke of—the one who was forgiven much but refused to forgive someone else (Matthew 18:21-35).

We tend to live with others by the letter of the law. Never forgiving, never overlooking. We judge people by how we would act, how we would think, how we would feel. And if they don't follow that pattern—our pattern—they are condemned. They are wrong. And left to ourselves, we are unbelievably hard on them because of those differences.

But not grace. Grace looks at the differences between people and accepts that when it comes to community—any community, whether marriage, family, neighborhood, workplace or church—differences are a reality. It's the way things are. It's something to be understood, not condemned. Even when those differences represent weakness—areas where someone may struggle profoundly with key issues of life. We see this in children's cruelty. They jump on any weakness in another and exploit it mercilessly. They taunt, they tease, they reject. Around easy targets—children who are overweight, wear braces, have a physical deformity, are not pretty or bright, or wear second-hand clothes—they're like sharks smelling blood in the water. When we get older, we do it differently, but the game is often the same. We instantly size people up, make assessments, and if a weakness presents itself, we can be merciless. Instead of grace, we pile on; particularly when it's in one of our areas of strength. Someone who is good with money has little patience or tolerance with someone who isn't. A naturally thin person can be harsh and cruel toward those who struggle with their weight. We typically understand weakness in another person if we share it. But in areas where we are strong, we have difficulty accepting weakness.

But grace understands that every human being is marked by weakness. When we lock eyes with others, we can safely assume that they carry deep wounds, have endured family dysfunction, live day-in and day-out with temptation and struggle. They are fragile and often broken.

And then it does something amazing.

Grace puts its arm around them.

The Bible says: "We who are strong ought to bear with the failings of the weak" (Romans 15:1). To "bear with" is not simply enduring, tolerating or putting up with someone. It lovingly upholds them, stands with them. Which is why that verse goes on to say, "Strength is for service, not status" (Romans 15:2 *The Message*).

But that's not all. Grace is to be applied to the most difficult place of all: someone else's sin. And specifically their sin against us. Most of us can look beyond a difference or a weakness, at least once we stop and think about it. But a sin? Particularly a sin that has been committed *against* us? Then we've really got something on them. They're guilty. And whatever we do, however we respond, is justified. *Because that's the penalty for sin.*

But here is the deep spiritual truth that must mark our faith, and our lives: Grace, by its very definition, is to be applied directly to someone else's sin. A bandage is designed to be applied to a cut. A contact lens is designed to be applied to an eye. Grace is to be applied to sin. That's God's design. That's what Jesus died for. Nowhere is this explained with more clarity than in the book of Romans. There the apostle Paul writes that sin doesn't "have a chance in competition with the aggressive forgiveness we call grace. When it's sin versus grace, grace wins hands down. . . . Grace . . . invites us into life" (Romans 5:20-21 *The Message*).

I've come to see with increasing clarity that more and more of us who consider ourselves Christ followers are somehow missing this truth. I know I miss it with unnerving frequency. Once I've identified something as a sin, a real wrong that has been done to me or that I've seen someone do to someone else, it's as if I have a license to turn grace off and condemn. It's as if that person can never be given another chance, is no longer deserving of consideration for anything good and is to be rejected and reviled. A kind of "one strike and you're out" mentality. Differences and weaknesses fine. But sin? No way!

But that's precisely what grace is for!

In truth, while we still live and breathe on this planet, grace has no limit, and nobody is ever out. Not that we ever condone or approve or make light of sin, but we have to get it into our heads that Christ died for *that very sin*. Refusing to extend grace emasculates the power and work of the cross. Community is, by definition, living with, interacting with, talking with, working with, being married to, parenting, even being pastored by a *sinner*. Sinful people who do all sorts of things that disturb us, hurt us, wound us. But grace interacts with that sin in a unique way. As C. S. Lewis noted, "To be a Christian means to forgive the inexcusable, because God has forgiven the inexcusable in you." But it goes beyond that—grace looks at the sin in others differently. Russian novelist Fyodor Dostoevsky wrote that grace heals our vision, letting us love people by seeing them as God intended them to be. Compare that to German philosopher Friedrich Nietzsche, who wrote in his autobiography of the ability to "smell" the inmost parts of every soul, especially the "abundant hidden dirt at the bottom" of a character. That is someone who mastered in ungrace. People of grace are more concerned with owning their own sin and overlooking it in others.

This is the mark of Christ.

And it should be the mark of a Christian.

- 6 -

POLARIZATIONS

MISPLACED MISSIONAL ENERGY

If they must be Christians,
let them at least be Christians with a difference.

SCREWTAPE

Comedian Emo Philips tells of walking across a bridge and seeing a man standing on the edge, ready to jump. He ran over and said, "Stop! Don't do it!"

"Why shouldn't I?" the man asked.

"Well, there's so much to live for."

"Like what?"

"Well, are you religious?"

He said yes.

Philips said, "Me too! Are you Christian or Buddhist?"

"Christian."

"Me too! Are you Catholic or Protestant?"

"Protestant."

"Me too! Are you Episcopalian or Baptist?"

"Baptist."

"Wow, me too! Are you Baptist Church of God or Baptist Church of the Lord?"

"Baptist Church of God!"

"Me too! Are you original Baptist Church of God or Reformed Baptist Church of God?"

"Reformed Baptist Church of God!"

"Me too! Are you Reformed Baptist Church of God, reformation of 1879, or Reformed Baptist Church of God, reformation of 1915?"

His new friend replied, "Reformed Baptist Church of God, reformation of 1915."

To which Philips replied, "Die, heretic!" and he pushed him off.

CHOOSING WAR

"Why is it that so often in theological controversy people seem to be so angry?" A. T. B. McGowan asks. In one respect, it's understandable that emotions run high. Theology deals with the most important subject matter of all—God—and thus surpasses every other matter of human concern. Humans, if nothing else, are contentious by nature. And it takes far less than God to bring those emotions to the surface.

It was just over 125 years ago, in Pike County, Kentucky, that a jury sentenced eight people to life in prison and ordered a ninth to be hanged for slaying four people.

All nine carried the name of Hatfield.

The four murdered were all McCoys.

Most of us have heard of the famous feud between these two clans. It's part of American folklore. The Hatfields, living mainly on the Virginia side of the Big Sandy River, and the McCoys, living in Pike County, Kentucky, fought on and off for a dozen years. Historians are not sure, but many estimate

Figure 6.1. The Hatfield Clan, 1897

that before it ended, up to twenty people died in their bloody little war. Some say the feud started in 1878 over a McCoy pig that ended up in a Hatfield pen. Others say that the dispute stemmed from the Civil War, in which the Hatfields fought for the Confederacy and the McCoys fought for the Union. Romanticists say the feud began over the secret love affair of Johnse Hatfield and Roseanna McCoy, who eventually bore him a child out of wedlock.

Whatever the cause, open warfare erupted in August 1882 when a member of the Hatfield clan was stabbed two dozen times and then shot in Pike County. The Hatfields subsequently kidnapped three McCoys and killed them all. The bitter conflict escalated until it reached its peak on New Year's Day 1888 when the Hatfields attacked the McCoy home on the Blackberry Fork of Pond Creek, burning it to the ground and killing two children. All over a pig, or at best, young love.

As Robert Corin Morris writes, of the various options when it comes to "the unity of the Spirit in the bond of peace" (Ephesians 4:3), one is war. War sets others apart as the enemy, often through a process of disrespect and dehumanization. Being at war and having enemies can be exhilarating. It brings a sense of moral clarity and purpose. The neat trick is that when we demonize our opponents, particularly when they are fellow Christians, we don't have to consider them Christian at all. We simply relegate them to a sub-Christian level and absolve ourselves of all responsibility for civility, much less charity. Unity is thus reduced to partisanship. With over nine thousand Christian denominations in the world, and six hundred in the United States alone, it is not difficult to see why we are so deeply polarized. What is less obvious is why Christ's call to relational unity is so easily discarded.

THE DIVIDES THAT DIVIDE

At this moment there are at least four major issues that are generating the most tension in evangelical Christianity: (1) Calvinism and Arminianism, (2) contemporary and more traditional approaches to ministry, (3) modern and postmodern sensibilities, and (4) activist opposition to private immorality versus civic concern with social justice and the environment.

Consider the tempest between traditional ministry and more contemporary approaches. An outsider might think this would be an honest debate about the most effective approach, weighing the value of new options against earlier methods. Instead, it often becomes a test of orthodoxy, such as the controversy that erupted in 2005 when Christmas Day fell on a Sunday, leading many more contemporary churches to scale back their services or even cancel them in light of the holiday. "This is a consumer mentality at work: 'Let's not impose the church on people. Let's not make church in any way inconvenient,'" sarcastically offered one seminary professor. "I think what this does is feed into the individualism that is found throughout American culture, where everyone does their own thing." Others chimed in: "What's going on here is a redefinition of Christmas as a time of family celebration rather than as a time of the community faithful celebrating the birth of the Savior. There is a risk that we will lose one more of our Christian rituals, one that's at the heart of our faith."

The truth is that evangelical churches of all kinds throughout the United States have seldom held services on Christmas Day when it has fallen on a Sunday (a tradition that dates back to the Puritans). Further, marking Christmas has never been tied to a Sunday-specific celebration (as with Easter). If there is a day that has uniformly been seized by churches to celebrate the birth of Christ, it has been Christmas Eve—and the churches being chastised for not having Sunday services on December 25 were planning on offering numerous services the night before.

The larger issue, of course, is how best to do ministry in our culture, pitting contemporary approaches against more traditional ones. Those who are already biased against contemporary methods seem eager to jump on anything that reflects an abandonment of tradition and thus, in their minds, orthodoxy. Those who are more contemporary immediately accuse their critics of confusing tradition with traditionalism, and thus spend little time explaining the biblical basis for their ministry choices.

The Christmas on Sunday issue was much ado about nothing and is easily diffused when differing parties are in relationship with each other and able to talk through their differences.

But the two sides aren't talking because they are so openly divided. Not just theologically but spiritually and emotionally. In fact, the entire debate took place in the media, happily enabled by reporters anxious for a fresh angle during a tired news cycle. And we seemed happy to parade our relational dysfunction in full view of the public.

And my fear is that we are headed for even worse behavior in the years to come.

For example, take what is perhaps the longest running of the four major divides, one that has increased in intensity in recent years—Calvinism versus Arminianism. Steve Lemke, provost of New Orleans Baptist Theological Seminary, publicly warns, "I believe that [Calvinism] is potentially the most explosive and divisive issue facing us in the near future." The theological divide between Calvinists and Arminians is an honest debate, and the matters are not without consequence. Yet like many such divides, it runs the risk of becoming less of an honest debate and more the grounds for open conflict.

It doesn't help that from the beginning this particular theological divide was laden with animus. Calvin himself, William Manchester writes, was considered "short-tempered and humorless. The slightest criticism enraged him." Whether an accurate portrayal of his disposition or not, those who questioned his theology he called "pigs," "asses," "riffraff," "dogs," "idiots" and "stinking beasts." In Geneva, where Calvin exerted his greatest influence, a denial of Calvin's understanding of predestination would result in banishment.

I am sure that similar lovelessness could be found among early Arminians.

There is little doubt that the Bible speaks about election and predestination, depravity and atonement, sovereignty and security. But thinking Christians have defined these terms in various ways. Calvin and Arminius offer two contrasting viewpoints. On Calvin's side we find such luminaries as B. B. Warfield, J. Gresham Machen and Charles Spurgeon; on the Arminian side, C. S. Lewis, Billy Graham and John Wesley. I am personally less concerned with determining who is right and who is wrong. Truth be told, we should have enough theologi-

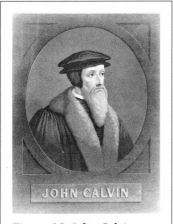

Figure 6.2. John Calvin

Figure 6.3. John Wesley (c. 1750-1791)

cal humility to admit that we all may be wrong. The greater issue is refusing to make our theological viewpoint the test of orthodoxy, the agenda for which we exist and the basis of our community.

And our rhetoric isn't helping.

When Calvinists say that Arminians believe in universalism, or Arminians say that Calvinists reject evangelism, we are not being fair. When one side or another lays claim to the term *Reformed*, as if the other is either Roman Catholic or against the Reformation ideals, we are not being accurate, as both flow from the Reformation. When we condescendingly say that our position is simply the "gospel," as if it's not really a debate worth having, then we are being arrogant. When we make our view the litmus test of orthodoxy, or even community, we are being neither gracious nor loving. When we say that our view alone upholds God's sovereignty or that our perspective is the only one that cares about lost people, we are not being truthful. When we exhibit a haughty smirkiness, or we so state our position that we divide churches, student ministry groups or denominations, then we are sinning.

THE VILLAGE GREEN

Coming from vastly different perspectives, Michael Horton, a Calvinist professor at Westminster Seminary, and Scot McKnight, an Anabaptist professor at North Park University, have both attempted to speak to evangelical differences in terms of the village green of early American communities, where folks gathered to chat and share their commonalities. Individual churches have well-defined statements of faith, and this is where we should join with Christians most like us in terms of faith and practice. But both Horton and McKnight agree that the local church (or denomination) is *not* the village green. The dilemma, McKnight observes, is when certain individuals or groups do not differentiate between the two. Instead, they want to make their confessions or particularities the gateway to the village green. Thus a particular tradition or stream of Christianity is elevated, almost to the status of Scripture. This is little more than fundamentalism at its worst. So for example, we must never equate the gospel with Calvin's theology, much less the views of Jacob Arminius.

John Stott writes about the importance of distinguishing between evangelical essentials, which cannot be compromised, and adiaphora (matters indifferent), which are not necessary.

Perhaps our criterion for deciding which is which . . . should be as follows. Whenever equally biblical Christians, who are equally anxious to understand the teaching of Scripture and to submit to its authority, reach different conclusions, we should deduce that evidently Scripture is not crystal clear in this matter, and therefore we can afford to give one another liberty.

Or as the seventeenth-century Lutheran Pietist Peter Meiderlin said, "In essentials, unity; in non-essentials, liberty; in all things, charity."

MISPLACED MISSIONAL ENERGY

What leads us to continually engage in such divides? If we can determine what fuels the endless polarizations, we might be able to move past the separations, at least relationally. I am convinced that there are three primary contributing factors, the first being misplaced missional energy.

When I speak of missional energy, I confess I have no verse to take you to, no great theological architect from history to cite, only a quarter of a century working with God's people as a pastor. But it is very real and must be considered. And when I speak to other pastors, they affirm its reality as well. It is as if there is a certain amount of missional energy within a community of faith, and it can be turned inward or outward. If turned outward toward authentic mission, the life of the community is relatively peaceful. There isn't the time or energy to focus on minor disagreements or petty arguments. No one cares what color the carpet is or the fine points of another's eschatology. They celebrate when a second Sunday school class is birthed from theirs. There are far larger issues at hand. However, energy not turned outward still exists. And when not spent on authentic mission, it turns on itself like a dog gnawing on its own leg. Suddenly miniscule matters of order, trivial variants of biblical interpretation, trifling questions about lifestyle come rushing to the fore with a sense of gravitas that is wickedly out of proportion.

THE PROBLEM OF PRIDE

The second dynamic fueling division is pride. As envy fuels much of our animus toward others on the personal front, pride does so on the macro level. As McGowan insightfully writes, "It is dreadfully simple to dress up our own arrogance and pride in the guise of 'defending the cause of the gospel.' "

Pride is more than simple vanity, which is a mere caricature of this sin. Vanity is a relatively benign trait that reduces self-absorption to lingering glances in the mirror and gratuitous boasts inserted into conversation. Vanity masks the real pitfall of pride, which arrogantly believes we can produce from our own imagination, our own resources or our own insights the standards and guidelines by which we will live. It's placing ourselves above any other source or authority that might speak to who we are, what we believe or how we should live. We assume the position of authority because we don't think anyone or anything else is truly superior to us. Pride plays to what we think we can do, what is biggest and best within us, which leads us to look down on everyone else. The more competent we consider ourselves to be, the more prideful we tend to become. When our sense of ability, knowledge or skill is believed to equal or surpass that of others, we refuse all counsel but our own. This is Dante's assessment. When he portrayed the proud of heart in hell, huge stones on their backs bend them over so they can't see anything but the ground. Since they looked down on everyone else in life, they were now unable to look up to see anything at all.

The antidote to pride is, of course, humility, and it is precisely humility which diffuses tension, bridges relational divides and brings Christian charity to bear on the most contentious of debates.

John Wesley, the founder of Methodism, and George Whitefield, a staunch Calvinist, were old college friends, having both attended Oxford. Both felt called into full-time vocational ministry, proclaiming the gospel at large, outdoor gatherings. Early on, their ministries ran on parallel tracks, with both enjoying wide acclaim. In fact, it was Whitefield who encouraged Wesley to begin his famed outdoor preaching.

But they soon grew apart theologically. Wesley embraced Arminianism and Whitefield Calvinism. But they remained warm and supportive friends even though they had profound disagreements.

Upon the death of Whitefield, Wesley—in compliance with Whitefield's request—preached his funeral sermon. Wesley was asked if he expected to see his old friend in heaven. Wesley's reply took the person by surprise: "No, [I won't see him in heaven] . . . [he'll] stand so near the throne of God that one like me will never catch a glimpse of him!"

THE FEAR FACTOR

But it isn't simply misplaced missional energy or pride that fuels our separations, but fear. We fear the different, the alien, the new, what we disagree with. And what we fear, we tend to isolate, demonize and attack.

One of the more glaring divides I faced as a pastor was the 2008 presidential election. I could feel the tension when a car with a "McCain-Palin" sticker pulled in next to one with "Obama-Biden" proudly adorning the bumper. What I sensed most was fear—fear of what would happen if one or the other won. Change was in the air no matter the results, and change is difficult.

I refused to have such things divide us. I wanted us to be able to talk openly about the issues, but I also knew that thinking Christians could land on different sides of many issues related to economics, the environment, human rights and war. Or at the very least, Christians divide on the best way to address these issues. We were one in Christ, and I wanted us to remain so. Even more to the point, regardless of who won the election, God was still on his throne. So before the election, I posted the following on my website—as much for my church as for anyone. It is simply a prayer for the president that I wanted to lead my people to embrace in the face of the fear.

Dear Mr. President:

I do not yet know your name, but in a few days you will be elected to our nation's highest office, and become the leader of the free world at the end of a long and engaging election season.

I wanted you to know that I will be praying for you. Not praying against you, or about you, but for you. That is both my pledge, and my obligation as a follower of Christ.

In the Bible, the apostle Paul writes, *"I urge, then, first of all, that requests, prayers, intercession and thanksgiving be made for everyone—for kings and all those in authority, that we may live peaceful and quiet lives in all godliness and holiness."*

And I will do so with a full and undivided heart.

I will be praying for you from my position as a father of four children, and God willing, future grandchildren; that you will have the foresight to think through what your decisions will mean for them as the next generation.

I will be praying for you as a citizen of the United States; that you will seek wisdom from God and humbly submit yourself to His leadership as you lead our nation through economic turbulence, domestic divides, and cultural diversities.

I will be praying for you as a member of the global population; that you will work with other well-intentioned leaders from around the world as we face environmental challenges, wars and rumors of wars, and humanitarian crises.

And finally, I will be praying for you as a Christian; that you will encourage faith in God to flourish and never allow deeply held spiritual convictions to become a matter of ridicule, instead encouraging everyone to grant them a respectful hearing, even if they go against the political policy of your party.

It is being widely spoken that the next president will inherit more that needs immediate attention than any other president in recent memory. As a result, it has been a hard-fought and hotly contested election. Yes, I will vote, and I do not know if you will be the one for whom I cast my ballot. But following November 4th, all that must be set aside no matter how deep the divides may be.

So while I do not know if you will be the candidate I voted for, I do know that no matter your name, I will support you in one way without question.

I will be praying for you.

Then, following the election of Barack Obama, I spoke to the church about the election. I called all in attendance to that spirit and to that prayer, no matter how they voted. I called them to celebrate the election itself, to celebrate the wonder of our democracy—young and old, rich and poor, white and black—freely casting their vote as a model to the world, particularly when the loser, in this case John McCain, offered such a quick and gracious congratulation to the victor, and pledged his support and prayers to his presidency. That simply doesn't happen in most countries. And this election was also set for history—we would either have our first African American president, forty years after the assassination of the leader of the civil rights movement, Martin Luther King Jr., or our first female vice president.

So as their pastor, I called them to treat the president of the United States with civility and respect, and to give him their prayers. That meant George Bush, as well as the president-elect Barack Obama. That was their duty as a follower of Christ.

Then I added these final words:

> Work for your beliefs. Make your convictions known. Join the political process, but never let yourself become so partisan that you become more of a Republican or a Democrat than a Christian. And never forget that as important as this election was, government pales in comparison to the church.

And particularly, its unity.

My goal was to lift their vision higher than the election, higher than who won or who lost, higher even than the world at hand and the small span of life on this earth. It is the only way past the fear—and once past the fear, the only way through to unity.

THE WALL IS THE CASTLE

There can certainly be reasoned and principled differences of opinion that sometimes, sadly, necessarily lead to separation. But what is plaguing the Christian community is lovelessness and pride, misplaced missional energy and fear, a war mentality and open hostility. It's as if we don't know how to agree to disagree *agreeably*. But even more, it's as if we don't realize what we are doing to ourselves, much less the cause of Christ. Perhaps it's because, as Frederick Buechner notes, anger is more fun.

> To lick your wounds, to smack your lips over grievances long past, to roll over your tongue the prospect of bitter confrontations still to come, to savor to the last toothsome morsel both the pain you are given and the pain you are giving back—in many ways it is a feast fit for a king.

Yet Buechner is wise in carrying the meal through to its final course. "The chief drawback," he continues, "is that what you are wolfing down is yourself. The skeleton at the feast is you."

One of the most contentious denominational gatherings in American ecclesial history took place in San Antonio, Texas, but many present felt it had more in common with the battle of Gettysburg than the standoff at the Alamo. It was the 1988 meeting of Southern Baptists, which drew nearly thirty-three thousand "messengers." I was one of them. Biblical inerrancy dominated discussions and deliberations.

W. A. Criswell, the revered pastor of First Baptist Church, Dallas, stepped to the podium and delivered what came to be known as the "skunk sermon" on the curse of liberalism. "A skunk by any other name still stinks," he warned. He was followed by the man who would soon be his successor at the church, Joel Gregory, who delivered a message titled "The Castle and the Wall," a desperate attempt to keep the denomination from fracturing.

Gregory told of a nobleman who had a castle that was continually being ravaged by scavengers. So he ordered a wall to be built around the castle to protect it. The workers asked the lord where the stones for the wall should be obtained, and the king declared, "What does that matter! Just build the wall!" Months later, the king visited his castle and found a large and imposing wall around the site of his castle. Once through the gate, he found his castle gone.

The workmen had gutted the castle for the stones needed to build the wall.

Gregory's point was to avoid defending the castle in such a way that the castle itself would be destroyed. Yes, the acrimony and animus surrounding the theo-

Figure 6.4. Ruins of the Sandal Castle, West Yorkshire, England

logical debate might produce a "winner," and a wall might be built, but at the expense of the castle. Gregory, and others like him, was not opposed to a wall—but not at the expense of the castle itself. Sadly, this is what many believe has happened to the Southern Baptist Convention, and many other churches, organizations and denominations like it, through a combination of fear, pride and misplaced missional energy.

Historian Bill Leonard of Wake Forest University presciently predicted that the acrimony of the Southern Baptist Convention would not dissipate once one side "won." It would simply turn its energies on another enemy, as the spirit of division knows no end. I mentioned there were thirty-three thousand delegates present in 1988. There were only six thousand present in 2008, with membership and baptisms in continual decline. And while inerrancy no longer dominates discussions, Calvinism, private prayer languages, alcoholic beverages and the viability of membership do.

OUR MOTHER

One, Holy, Catholic, Apostolic

You cannot have God as your father
unless you have the church for your mother.

CYPRIAN OF CARTHAGE

Near the beginning of my rather short tenure as a seminary president, I sat in the boardroom of a prominent Christian business leader to pitch a vision for contributing to theological education, specifically student scholarships. Instead of listening to the opportunity or asking pertinent questions about the value of such an investment, he was determined to boast of his company's identity as a Christian enterprise. He told of the mission trips he had taken with his employees, the investments the company had made from its profits in select boutique parachurch ventures, and the Bible study offered on campus for employees. Throughout his self-congratulatory spiel he took more than his fair share of shots at local churches and pastors who were not as "alive" as he and his company were in their faith. Forgive me, but he was insufferably full of his own spiritual self-importance and virtue, as if he had drunk a bit too deeply from the fawning of countless pilgrims who had come to his corporate offices to laud his beneficence and ask for his generosity.

Like me.

At the time, as a new seminary president facing an inherited budgetary shortfall of over one million dollars, I was willing to endure almost anything—or anyone—for aid. I smiled and nodded, affirming his many self-ascribed accolades. Then, in the midst of one of his personal asides about the sorry state of the church as compared to the pristine missional nature of his business, he maintained that it was for this reason that he wasn't involved in a local church. They were, he intimated, beneath his own theological vision. "And after all," he added, "we're the church too."

And then everything within me wanted to leap from my seat, shout "Enough!" and say, "No, you are *not!*" A company is *not* the body of Christ instituted by Jesus as the hope of the world, chronicled breathtakingly by Luke through the book of Acts, and shaped in thinking and practice by the apostle Paul through letter after letter now captured in the New Testament. A marketplace venture on the New York Stock Exchange is not so expansive with energy that not even the gates of hell can withstand its onslaught. An assembly of employees in cubicles working for end-of-year stock options and bonuses is not the gathering of saints bristling with spiritual gifts and mobilizing to provide justice for the oppressed, service to the widow and the orphan, and compassion for the poor.

But it is not surprising that an evangelical, Bible-believing follower of Christ would think that it is. The research of D. Michael Lindsay on the leaders of evangelical Christianity found that among Christian presidents and CEOs, senior business executives and Hollywood icons, celebrated artists and world-class athletes, more than half had low levels of commitment to their congregations. Some were members in name only; others had actively disengaged from church life.

With jaw-dropping vigor, ignorance and at times unblushing gall, increasing sectors of the evangelical world are abandoning two thousand years of ecclesiology (the doctrine of the church) as if the church was some malleable human construct that can be shaped, altered, redefined or even disposed of as desired. This, coupled with a radical revisionism in biblical interpretation and ecclesial history more in line with *The Da Vinci Code* than Christian theology, and you have the doctrine of the church being reformulated apart from biblical moorings or simply dismissed as if not a part of biblical orthodoxy at all.

For example, it is more than disturbing that a recent survey of American Christians found that the majority deemed each of the following to be "a complete and biblically valid" way for someone who does not participate in a conventional church to experience and express their faith in God:

- engaging in faith activities at home
- watching a religious television program
- listening to a religious radio broadcast
- attending a special ministry event, such as a concert or community service activity
- participating in a marketplace ministry

But as the early church father Cyprian maintains, "You cannot have God as your father unless you have the church for your mother."

THE BANE OF THE REFORMATION

So what happened? In many ways the answer is that the Reformation happened. As a Protestant, I obviously believe much within the Reformation was both needed and good. But there was much that flowed from the Reformation that was neither. Specifically, a loss of historical sense and a robust ecclesiology.

Too often Protestant Christians seems to think that the Reformation was the beginning of the Christian faith instead of a turning point within its history. Church history did not begin with Luther posting his ninety-five theses on the door of the Wittenberg church on October 31, 1517. If we believe it did, we divorce ourselves from a rich heritage that would, among many other things, speak to a strong ecclesiology. Robert Webber, known for championing the patristic era, used to tell of a colleague at Wheaton College who said, "Webber, you act like there never was a Reformation." To which Bob replied, "You act like there never was an ancient church." Failing to recognize this long and rich history "is to be stripped of our story, heritage, and even identity," writes Kenneth Collins, who then added, "Stripped and naked is no way in which to enter the twenty-first century."

Among evangelicals this truncated view of history has been a double-edged sword. For most it has led to a trivialization of the church; for a growing minority it has led to a hunger for a deeper sense of church than they found in their evangelical upbringing. This hunger, coupled with the lost sense of history, has led many to feel the need to leave evangelical Christianity in order to tap into the rich narrative of ancient and medieval faith, putting many evangelicals on the Canterbury trail toward Anglicanism or even leading them to "cross the Tiber" into Catholicism. I'm not suggesting that one cannot be an evangelical Anglican or an evangelical Catholic. But many are driven to this, often at the expense of true theological conviction, by their desire for the biblical vision for the church—or any vision for the church.

Adding to the ecclesial wasteland was the attempt by many Reformers to purify the church from its medieval excesses. My seminary patristics professor used to quip that Calvin reduced the church to "four walls and a Bible." It wasn't that strong of an exaggeration. Evidence of the ferocious assault on all things "Rome" can be found throughout Europe. I recall walking through Holyrood Palace at the foot of the Royal Mile in Edinburgh, Scotland, which was founded as a monastery in 1128, and seeing rows of empty alcoves once filled with precious art

Figure 7.1. Holyrood Abbey, Bristol, United Kingdom

that had been destroyed by the Scottish Protestant leader John Knox's inspiration of a "rascal multitude" in 1567. Or more recently walking through St. George's Basilica in the Prague Castle in the Czech Republic, which was decimated by radical Calvinists who felt they had to destroy priceless art in order to make the church suitable for Protestant worship. A wood relief in the church chronicles the debasement.

The point is that if we look to the Reformation alone, our

vision of the church is often depleted by the excesses of Reformation frenzy.

The Reformation didn't just spawn a rejection of medieval ecclesiology. As it wrenched itself from the monolithic nature of the Catholic church, it spawned the birth of free-market spiritual entrepreneurialism, which in turn weakened ecclesiology even more, particularly as it later washed upon the shores of the American continent. If there is a dominant force shaping the contours of American Christianity, it is, without a doubt, democratization. Historian Nathan Hatch notes that the democratic spirit deeply affected popular religious movements—and especially evangelicalism—in three respects. First, it denied the age-old distinction that set the clergy apart from all others. Anyone could "minister." They did not need to work through a church or ecclesiastical body. Second, ordinary people were empowered to take their deepest spiritual impulses at face value rather than subjecting them to the scrutiny of orthodox doctrine or an ecclesial body. Further, those who chose to minister did not have to be subject to oversight. The democratization of American Christianity is the story of "how ordinary folk came to . . . defend the right of common people to shape their own faith and submit to leaders of their own choosing." So not only were leaders turned loose, but so were the followers. Third, the people had little if any sense of limitations. They dreamed that a new age of religious and social harmony could flow from their efforts.

And democratization took hold. To be sure, as Hatch also notes, the free-market mindset helped to ensure the vitality of American faith. But apart from a clear and ongoing understanding *of* and commitment *to* the biblical and historical idea of the church, it soon gave rise to a collection of parachurch and freelance ministries that separated ministry from a theology of the church. Or more to the point, from church in general. And in many ways the worst of the parachurch movement continues to undermine a robust view of the role and ministry of the church.

Let me state the obvious. A parachurch ministry, InterVarsity Christian Fellowship—and specifically InterVarsity Press—is the publisher of this book. Further, I became a Christ follower through this very same parachurch group while a twenty-year-old college student. I am indebted to its ministry, and I attempt to give back to it at every opportunity.

Yet the critique of the parachurch movement as a whole, with notable exceptions, remains.

THE PARACHURCH MOVEMENT

The word *parachurch* is built of two words: *para*, which means "alongside of," and *church*. As conceived, the parachurch is meant to serve alongside the church, not in place of or in competition with the church. One could easily trace its roots to the early monastic movement and countless subsequent ministry endeavors since. Originally embraced as a way to enlarge the boundaries of God's work beyond the traditional church, it has often become a substitute entity, sometimes competitive and occasionally antagonistic. The role of the parachurch has loomed so large in certain circles that it has led some to speak of the potential partnership of the church and parachurch, as if it might be a nice option, which reveals the devaluation of our ecclesiology.

Lest what I write be misconstrued, as mentioned, I became a follower of Christ through a parachurch ministry, so I am deeply indebted to the fruit that can flow from parachurch efforts. And there are many legitimate and even strategic parachurch ministries.

But there are many that are not.

Many parachurch ministries began at the invitation of the local church, but when the church proper was prepared to fully do what the parachurch ministry was asked to do, the parachurch ministry refuses to close up shop or move elsewhere. Thus it no longer serves alongside the church, but rather requests others to "pay, pray and get out of the way."

When a parachurch group does little more than replicate what local churches are doing, it is not a healthy enterprise. This is precisely what we have with countless parachurch efforts.

The free-market response is to point to success, to results alone, and from that claim biblical justification. But just because Jim Bakker raised a lot of money during a telethon in Clearwater, Florida, on the day of his sexual tryst with a secretary, it didn't make his ministry legitimate. Though the Bible says to make judgments based on fruit, it is a common misinterpretation to assume this means legitimacy. The fruit the Bible has in mind is the fruit of the Spirit. Some parachurch groups are justified in light of their relationship with the church, and some are not, success notwithstanding. But whether legitimate or not, parachurch groups are *not* the church, nor should they become a substitute for the church.

So where *is* the church today? When do you know the church is truly present? Is a campus group the church? Is a small group the church? As a pastor, such matters are far from academic. Knowing what is and is not the church is often at the heart of daily life. Consider these scenarios:

- the energetic young man who makes an appointment, casts a vision for a parachurch marketplace ministry, and wants the church to support his efforts and platform his seminars

- the small group that asks if they can take the Lord's Supper together

- the homeschooling family who asks about "home-churching"
- the father who wants to baptize his son in his backyard pool
- the opportunity to offer satellite campuses with video teaching throughout the city and even around the world
- the volunteer who is interested in leadership, but does not want to become a member

Precisely these kinds of practical questions drive us to strengthen our grip on knowing when we do have and are being the church.

THE NATURE OF THE CHURCH

The biblical word for church is *ecclesia*, which literally means "the called-out ones." *Ecclesia* was used in Jesus' day for any group that was gathered together for a specific purpose or mission. Jesus seized the term to speak of a group with a *very* specific purpose or mission, setting it apart from every other group or mission. The church of Christ, however, is anything but a man-made organization; it was founded and instituted by Jesus himself (Matthew 16:18).

In the Bible there are three primary understandings of the church, the body of Christ: (1) the local church, (2) the universal church as it exists around the world, and (3) the church as it exists throughout history, comprising all of the saints past, present and future. Without question the dominant biblical use is to a local church or collection of local churches. Think of how the letters of Paul were written: "To the church of God at Corinth," "To the churches in Galatia," "To the church of the Thessalonians," and at the beginning of John's Revelation, "To the seven churches in the province of Asia."

This church was to serve as the ongoing manifestation of Christ on earth, being called his "body," an idea of profound significance throughout the New Testament. As the apostle Paul wrote: "Just as each of us has one body with many members, and these members do not all have the same function, so in Christ we who are many form one body, and each member belongs to all the others. We each have different gifts, according to the grace given us" (Romans 12:4-6). And later in the New Testament we read Paul reiterating this idea: "Now you are the body of Christ, and each one of you is a part of it" (1 Corinthians 12:27). And if the point hadn't been made clearly enough, Paul writes the following words to the church at Ephesus: "And God placed all things under [Christ's] feet and appointed him to be head over everything for the church, which is his body, the fullness of him who fills everything in every way" (Ephesians 1:22-23; see also Ephesians 5:23; Colossians 1:18; 2:19). Beyond the interconnectedness this suggests, it means that the church is the locus of Christ's activity, and he works through the church now as he worked through his physical body during

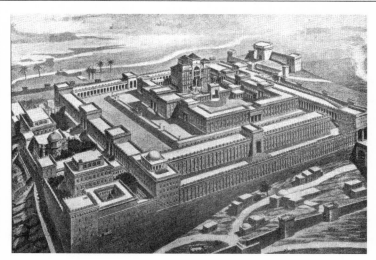

Figure 7.2. Temple of Solomon in Jerusalem

his life on earth. In the New Testament there is no ministry outside of the church, or at least its umbrella.

But what is this "local" church that functions as the body of Christ?

ONE, HOLY, CATHOLIC, APOSTOLIC

The earliest church, in the first forty or so years following the resurrection of Jesus, was essentially a movement within Judaism that believed the Messiah had come. But then, around A.D. 70, Jerusalem fell to the Romans, and the Christian church was dispersed. One of the most important churches to emerge, as you would imagine, was the one in Rome, which was the capital of the Roman Empire.

During the next few centuries, the church defined itself by four very important words: *one*, *holy*, *catholic* and *apostolic*. Each word carries great significance. First, the church is to be *one*, or unified. Jesus, in his grand final prayer recorded in John's Gospel, prayed fervently for unity among those who would embrace his name in the centuries to come. Second, the church is to be *holy*, meaning set apart for God and separate from the world, for God himself is holy. Third, the church is to be *catholic*, which means "universal." The church is to be a worldwide church, one that includes all believers under its umbrella. (Note that the word *catholic* was used of the church long before the Roman Catholic Church.) Finally, the church is to be *apostolic*, which means committed to the teaching handed down by Jesus through the apostles.

Beyond being one, holy, catholic and apostolic, local churches have definition and form, structure and purpose. They are not simply doing "community" in the broadest sense, much less simply pursuing ministry. In the Bible, the church is a defined, purposeful gathering of believers who know they are coming together to *be* a church. There are defined entry and exit points to the church, clear theological guidelines navigating corporate and community waters, the responsibility of stewarding the sacraments, specifically named leadership positions, and a singular mission. Yes, we often hear that the church is where "the Gospel is rightly taught and the sacraments rightly administered." This is taken from the Augsburg Confession (1530), the primary Lutheran confessional statement, courtesy of Martin Luther and Philip Melanchthon. Calvin said much the same thing in his *Institutes of the Christian Religion* (4.1.9). But sensing the inadequacy of such a definition, in 1539 Luther wrote *On the Councils and the Church*, adding five more distinguishing characteristics, including church discipline, ordination, and worship through prayer and singing.

Unfortunately, there are those who intimate that the idea of the church in the New Testament is either so embryonic or ethereal that we have the freedom to define the church as we wish. This simply is not the case. In trying to convey the specificity inherent within the nature and definition of the church to my seminary students, including a clear sense of when we know we actually have the church in operation and not just a pale imitation or even impostor, I came up with five "Cs."

COMMUNITY

To be a church, we must be a community of faith. This community should not be segmented in any way, whether by race, ethnicity, gender or age. In fact, the radical declaration of Paul in Galatians is that in Christ such divisions must no longer exist (Galatians 3:28). There is clear instruction that such divisions are to be turned on their head: the young are not to be despised when called to lead their elders (1 Timothy 4:12), and the wealthy should care for those without (Acts 2:45). While those outside of the faith are to be welcomed and spiritually served, they don't constitute the church itself and must not partake in its sacraments. As a defined community of faith, we read how the New Testament church had clear entry and exit points. We see this throughout the New Testament, not only in the address of Paul's letters to defined groups of people in various geographic locations, but also in the prescribed exercise of church discipline. Paul speaks of those "inside" and "outside" the church, and stresses the importance of expelling those who are wicked and unrepentant (1 Corinthians 5:12-13).

CONFESSION

The second dynamic constituting the church is *confession*. In this context confession is related to the Greek *homologeō,* which means "to say the same thing" or "to agree." For the church to

Figure 7.3. The Council in Nicaea, A.D. 325

be the church, it must be a place where the Word of God, Scripture, is proclaimed in its fullness. If a Christian church is anything, it is foundationally *confessional*, for the earliest mark of the Christian movement was the clear confession that Jesus is the Christ (Mark 8:29) and the Lord (Romans 10:9; see also Acts 16:31; 1 Corinthians 12:3; Philippians 2:11).

Formal confessions of faith, which are doctrinal summaries of essential Christian beliefs, have been developed throughout the history of the Christian church in order to standardize basic doctrinal commitments. Among the earliest of examples is the Creed of Nicaea, so called because it is based on the deliberations of the Council of Nicaea (A.D. 325):

> We believe in one God the Father All-sovereign, maker of all things visible and invisible;
>
> And in one Lord Jesus Christ, the Son of God, begotten of the Father, only-begotten, that is, of the substance of the Father, God of God, Light of Light, true God of true God, begotten not made, of one substance with the Father, through whom all things were made, things in heaven and things on the earth; who for us men and for our salvation came down and was made flesh, and became man, suffered, and rose on the third day, ascended into the heavens, is coming to judge living and dead.
>
> And in the Holy Spirit.
>
> And those that say "there was when he was not,"
>
> > and, "Before he was begotten he was not,"
> >
> > and that, "He came into being from what-is-not,"
>
> or those that allege, that the son of God is
>
> > > "Of another substance or essence"
> > >
> > > or "created"
> > >
> > > or "changeable"
> > >
> > > or "alterable,"
>
> these the Catholic and Apostolic Church anathematizes.

CORPORATE

The third mark of the church is *corporate*. The Bible speaks of defined organizational roles, such as pastors/elders/bishops/

deacons, as well as corporate roles related to spiritual gifts such as teachers, administers and leaders (Romans 12; 1 Corinthians 12; Ephesians 4; 1 Peter 4). These corporate dynamics allowed money to flow from one group to another (2 Corinthians 8), decisions to be made by leaders regarding doctrine and practice (Acts 15), and the setting apart of some individuals for appointed tasks, mission and church plants (Acts 13). There are often disparaging quips made about "organized religion," but there was nothing disorganized about the biblical model.

CELEBRATION

The fourth dynamic of the local church is *celebration*. The church is to gather for public worship as a unified community of faith, which includes the stewarding of the sacraments of baptism and the Lord's Supper, for these were not in the public domain. In the New Testament, believers were to "come together" for the Supper, and its proper administration fell under apostolic teaching and direction, which was then delegated to pastors to oversee. Indeed, refusing church members' participation in the Lord's Supper by church leaders has been one of the more common approaches to church discipline throughout history.

CAUSE

The final mark of the local church relates to *cause*. Jesus has given the church a very specific mission to reach out to a deeply fallen world and call it back to God. According to the Bible this involves active evangelism with subsequent discipleship, coupled with strategic service to the needy. We are to be the body of Christ to the world, and the twin dynamics of evangelism and social concern reflect Christ's ongoing mission. This cause may be the most defining mark of all. Theologian Jürgen Moltmann reminds us that the church does not *have* a mission; rather, the mission *has* us. And the mission of Christ creates the church. God sent his Son, and now sends us. This is the *missio Dei*, the "sending of God." As Christopher J. H. Wright contends, our mission "means our committed participation as God's people, at God's invitation and command, in God's own mission within the history of God's world for the redemption of God's creation." So the mission of God and the church are inextricably intertwined.

There is a phrase that runs in some circles. When a glimpse of Christ's dream erupts, they exclaim, "This is church!" Much of it flows from asides within Luke's Acts narrative, where he seems to pause his history, full of the drama of the unfolding of Christ's dream, and writes a description of the church's power and majesty. Perhaps his most well-known summation is in the second chapter:

> They devoted themselves to the apostles' teaching and to the fellowship, to the breaking of bread and to prayer. Everyone was filled with awe, and many wonders and miraculous signs were done by the apostles. All the believers were together and had everything in common. Selling their possessions and goods, they gave to anyone as he had need. Every day they continued to meet together in the temple courts. They broke bread in their homes and ate together with glad and sincere hearts, praising God and enjoying the favor of all the people. And the Lord added to their number daily those who were being saved. (Acts 2:42-47)

This is church! It was a beautiful thing to behold. The challenge is to so pursue it that we might behold it again.

- 8 -

THE CHURCH UNHINDERED

It's Not About Me

*I will put together my church, a church so expansive with energy
that not even the gates of hell will be able to keep it out.*

MATTHEW 16:18 *THE MESSAGE*

It's down, it's out—and its core voters are getting old." So
opened a recent *Newsweek* article on the Republican party. "If
the GOP expects to rebound, it had better figure out how to
reach younger voters. But how?" For fun, *Newsweek* asked four
hot, nonpartisan design firms to tackle the job.

The New York–based Pentagram agency submitted "Renew.
Reinvest. Refresh. Recommit. Restore. Rethink. Republican."

Frog Design, also out of New York, offered the idea of the
party initiating a national brainstorming session, along the
lines of "A New Vision for America 2012."

Razorfish, out of Chicago, suggested that to reach new voters, you have to speak "tech." As a result, they counseled the
GOP to become smart users of social media, such as investing
in a strong social networking site. Or even more forward-
thinking, an iPhone application that allowed users to register

friends without ever touching a piece of paper.

The Groop, of Los Angeles, encouraged a new lexicon. Out: "old money" and "faith-based." In: "new wealth" and "spirituality-based."

I couldn't help but wonder, What if *Newsweek* had asked four leading agencies to brainstorm for American Christianity? On the surface, it would be a welcomed effort. Studies show the image of Christianity in America is in shambles: we are considered hypocritical, judgmental, unloving, homophobic and far too involved in politics. But in the end, nothing is solved through mere "surface rebranding." I often speak with pastors of struggling churches who feel this is the answer. They want to change their church's name, update their website or move to a new location. It never quite enters their mind that perhaps their worship experience or the quality of their messages is lacking, or they have a dysfunctional community, or they have lost sight of the missional task inherent within the Great Commission. Finding a marketing breakthrough is not the goal. Lest we forget, to preach the cross in the first century was to preach shame, humiliation and scandal. As Sean McDonough writes, "when Paul made the cross the centerpiece of his preaching, he was arguably making *the single worst marketing decision in the history of mankind.*"

What was the secret of the early church? Simple. It so incarnated the gospel that it overcame its market weakness and stormed the hearts of a deeply pagan culture.

Simply put, it went on mission.

So how do we resurrect the Christian brand?

We resurrect the church.

A PERSONAL PILGRIMAGE

I never wanted to pastor a church.

I didn't give my life to Christ until I was a sophomore in college, and though at that time I felt a desire to give my life in some way to the cause of Christ, the church never entered my mind. Based on everything I knew and had experienced, the church just wasn't where it was happening. When I looked at the church, I saw a bunch of dead, stagnant, graying organizations that were about as far from the cutting edge of making an impact as can be imagined. To me, the church was optional. It was marginal, just another human organization, the epitome of organized religion, which I wanted nothing to do with. Church was for old ladies and kids, organs and potluck suppers.

Whatever church was, it wasn't changing the world. It was the last thing I could imagine giving my life to.

I had been reached for Christ by friends who invited me to a campus outreach event led by a group of twentysomethings who used contemporary music and practical communicators to connect with college kids. My heroes quickly became Christian authors and thinkers who were engaging the world and making a difference for Christ in the public square of ideas, culture and commerce. So when I went to seminary for my master of divinity degree and then my Ph.D. in theology, biblical studies and history, I intended to spend my life in scholarship, writing and speaking at a university or seminary.

But during graduate school, just before I began my doctoral work, I received a call from a church near the school asking me to be their interim pastor. It was an established denominational church in a county-seat town near the seminary. I didn't want to serve in a church, much less be a pastor, but for a whole host of deeply spiritual reasons—they were going to *pay* me—I felt it was something I should do. And it turned into a full-fledged call to serve as their senior pastor. I said yes again. After all, this time the pay included a parsonage. But by *saying* yes I was introduced to what seemed to be one of the most dysfunctional

churches in history, and it was one of the most emotionally trying times of my life. Even now, after all these years, it is not
easy to bring back to mind. At the time the church was full of
division and discord, broken relationships and power plays,
malicious gossip and slander, biting criticism and petty sensi-
tivities. Suffice it to say, the spirit pervading the church bore
little reflection of the Spirit. I should have seen the writing on
the wall when I discovered that I was the fourth pastor they had
in less than ten years. But I was young and didn't know how to
read those kinds of signs.

After about a year I called the former pastors (at the time, I
did not know this was not often done) and found out that the
pastor who preceded me had had an emotional breakdown and
actually collapsed during a service. He was given a sabbatical,
which he promptly used to find a new position in Florida. The
pastor before him told me he had been run off by a deacon in
the church. This deacon had gone to the parsonage one evening
to tell the pastor that it was time for him to move on, and if he
didn't, the deacon would make it so hard for the pastor that he'd
have to leave.

So there I was—extremely young for the role, no experience,
trying to finish up my Ph.D., with no desire to pastor or serve a
church in the first place—right in the middle of a nightmare. I
would get a pit in my stomach, like I was sitting in a dentist's
chair, every time I drove to the church. But the church wasn't
just dysfunctional relationally; it was more than that. The members had been reaching hardly anyone for Christ. There was
virtually no sense of worship. Few had been growing in their
faith and becoming more like Jesus. Scant needs had been met
through ministry.

It was as if I was being given a front-row seat to everything
that was wrong with the church today.

Two things happened to me during the three years I pastored that church. First, as you might imagine, I became more convinced than ever that I didn't want to be a pastor. There was no way I could live that way. I couldn't last in that environment, and even more, I could not imagine submitting my family to such emotional trauma. It's one thing to take a hit *for* the kingdom; it's another to take one *from* the kingdom.

But a second thing happened at the same time, something that completely and totally blindsided me. While I was in the midst of that trying experience, I began to fall in love with the *idea* of church, the *vision* of church, the church that *Jesus* came to establish—the new community he talked about that is compellingly described in the Bible. In the New Testament, the church was a place where people devoted themselves to spiritual growth, and it changed their life. They were in deep community with each other, the kind where they were knowing and being known, loving and being loved. They were meeting needs in each other's lives and in the lives of those around them. They were worshiping God deeply, from the heart, and celebrating him. They took their faith to and made a difference in the marketplace—outliving, outthinking and outserving the world. And they were reaching out to those who did not know God, who were far from Christ, with the one message that would change the entire trajectory of their life. As I read the Bible and studied what it had to say, I became convinced that the church was what Christ came to establish as *the* intended means for ministry in the world. He wanted to change the world and to do it through the church.

The tension in my life and heart was palpable. After a brutal day of trying to serve in the context of a church that had a trail of pastors' bodies in its wake, I would lie awake at night and dream about what church could be and should be like. I would have conversations with my wife that would start off with "Wouldn't church be great *if* . . ." "Can you imagine what would happen if we could just do *this?*" I didn't know it at the time, but the Holy Spirit's Acts 2 vision was gaining an increasing grip on my life: *What if the church could be the church?*

After graduation, I was invited to become the National Leadership Consultant for Preaching and Worship for the largest Protestant denomination in the United States. (I would say "Southern Baptist," but I don't want to lose you!) My job was to study the nation's most gifted communicators, the fastest-growing churches, the most innovative approaches to ministry, and then teach and write about them to the denomination. I could order any book, buy any recording, travel to any site, have access to virtually any leader. It was the education no one gets in seminary.

I recall visiting Trabuco Hills High School in Mission Viejo, California, as a young Rick Warren walked among folding chairs set up for the fledgling Saddleback Valley Community Church (and eating Thai food with him later). I recall connecting with Bill Hybels in South Barrington, Illinois, long before there was a Willow Creek Association, over a lunch in the bridal room by the chapel. Through these and countless other encounters, the vision began to change from "What if the church could be the church" to seeing the vision fleshed out. I asked myself, *What if, with my one and only life, I could experience the church being the church?* I was beginning to catch glimpses, in high schools and movie theaters, and through new approaches and initiatives, of the dynamic reality of the church. It wasn't long before the person who never wanted to pastor a church began to see the church as the hope of the world, and that there is nothing that I could give my life to that would matter more.

I've been chasing that vision ever since.

IDEA AND IDEAL

I know that many, if not most, Christians have become disillusioned with the church. As Katie Galli once noted about her fellow twentysomethings,

> We're disillusioned about almost everything—government, war, the economy. . . . We're *especially* disillusioned with the church. Somewhere between the Crusades, the Inquisition, and fundamentalists bombing abortion clinics, we lost our appetite for institutionalized Christianity.

I understand.

But the church *is* an institution and needs to be. And while "the church can indeed be bureaucratic, inefficient, and, at times, hopelessly outdated," Galli wisely adds, "it has also given us a 2,000-year legacy of saints and social reformers, and a rich liturgy and theology—the very gift 20-somethings need to grow into the full stature of Christ." But this is far from a generational

Figure 8.1. Antigay protest in San Francisco

challenge. Aging baby boomer Philip Yancey writes of his estrangement from the church, noting how the hypocrisy of the members and the cultural irrelevance of its experience kept him away for years. Why did he return? "Christianity is not a purely intellectual, internal faith. It can only be lived in community."

Ironically, the real dilemma with the church is not the church itself but the staggering power of the biblical vision *for* the church. Christ's dream for the church is so strong, so compelling, so vibrant that the pale manifestation on the corner of Elm and Vine can breed disdain. As Sarah Cunningham writes,

> I have been and continue to be frustrated when Christian religious systems seem to fall short of the community God intended his followers to experience. However, my belief in the ideal of church—in God's design for those who align themselves with him—is uncompromised.

But the telling statement comes later when she owns the rampant idealism that pervades her generation's approach to all of life: "It's no surprise, then, that twentysomethings tend to apply these same idealistic ideas to a search for the perfect church. When we don't find perfection, we can start to get a bit antsy."

Any ideal can act in two ways: it can drive us toward its fulfillment or away from its pursuit entirely, in disappointment. Sadly, many are choosing to leave the vision in disappointment. They remain loyal to the idea of church but not its practice, citing the chasm between the vision and the reality as their rationale. This is understandable and is precisely what plagued me in my twenties. But there is a new dynamic to the idealism of our day, which has become pandemic. If we are to resurrect the Christian "brand" by resurrecting the church, there is one thing that we will have to die to.

Ourselves.

IT'S NOT ABOUT ME

The names say it all: YouTube. MySpace. And, of course, the "i" in iPod, iTunes, iMac and iPhone. When *Time* magazine searched for the person of the year for 2007, which in the past has been filled with presidents, dictators, business moguls and religious leaders, they chose "You." The cover sported a mylar mirror so that readers could see their reflection. Certainly, today's theme is "It's all about me." Tom Wolfe had earlier labeled the 1970s the "Me Decade." But Jean M. Twenge writes that compared to today's generation, the seventies generation "were posers."

Figure 8.2. Painting of Narcissus by Caravaggio, c. A.D. 1573-1610

In Greek mythology, Narcissus is the character who, upon passing his reflection in the water, becomes so enamored with himself that he devotes the rest of his life to observing his own reflection. From this we get our term *narcissism*, the preoccupation with self. The narcissistic "I, me, mine" mentality places personal pleasure and fulfillment at the forefront of concerns. Historian Christopher Lasch went so far as to christen ours "the culture of narcissism," saying that this is the new religion—a religion where we don't actually want religion proper, but instead, personal therapy.

And this spirit has invaded our thinking and is at war with the church.

Eavesdrop, for a moment, on our Christian rhetoric. "I want to go where I'm fed"—not where we can learn to feed ourselves, much less feed others. "I need to be ministered to," as if ministry is something that happens to us, instead of something we make happen for others. We walk out of a worship service and say, "I didn't get anything out of it," as if that was its purpose—our edification, instead of God's. This consumer mindset looks at the church in terms of how it caters to specific felt needs. This from a people whose Savior said, "I did not come to be served, but to serve, and to give my life as a ransom for many." A Savior who said, "Whoever wants to be first must become last." A Savior who said, "Whoever wants to be great among you must become the slave of all." A Savior who said to the Father, "Not my will, but thine." Yet a *spiritual* narcissism has invaded our thinking; the individual needs and desires of the believer have become the center of attention.

When rampant idealism meets a consumer mindset that rests on a weak ecclesiology, we have the proverbial "perfect storm," and the church is cast aside and trampled on as so much refuse.

Saint Cyprian once famously declared *Nulla salus extra ecclesiam*—apart from, or outside of, the church, there is no salvation. While this is fraught with theological baggage, the lowest common denominator of assent would affirm that we cannot come to Christ without also coming to his church. We have made spirituality far too individualistic, failing to realize that something such as salvation is not a private affair. When I come to Christ, it is not simply between me and Jesus. It is between me and his body, the church. Mind you, salvation does not reside in the church, but it cannot be bracketed off as something immaterial. As John Stott writes of the Holy Spirit's work in the early church, "He 'added to their number . . . those who were being saved.' He didn't add them to the church without saving them, and he didn't save them without adding them to the church. Salvation and church membership went together; they still do."

ECCLESIA MILITANS

The heart of the matter is that we are on mission for Christ, and the heart of that mission is the church. Not simply in and through the church, but the church itself as it fulfills Christ's vision and reaches its redemptive potential. The church exists as the body of Christ to the world, living as he lived, serving as he served, sacrificing as he sacrificed. As Jesus said, "The Son of Man did not come to be served, but to serve, and to give his life as a ransom for many" (Mark 10:45). This is the reason for the Latin phrase *ecclesia militans*, which describes the church as it is *now* engaged in spiritual warfare, as opposed to the *ecclesia triumphans*, or "church triumphant," which is the church blessed, or at rest, both now and in eternity. We are the "ecclesia," called out, gathered, in order to be *militant*.

When we talk of someone being militant, or militantly against something, we think of someone on the warpath—usually in a distasteful way. But the word simply means to serve as a soldier. As militants, we are on active duty as part of a military. We are part of a war, a conflict, a great struggle—and we must be ready to join with others to fight in whatever way needed. According to Jesus, the church is *the* heart of the force of God on this planet. He wants to change the world, and he wants to do it through the church. And the more the church is gathered, the more the church is focused, the more it pulls together the collective energies of God's people, the more powerful and influential it becomes.

Think about how this works with light. Light that is diffused doesn't make much difference. But when light is focused through a magnifying glass, it can set things on fire. Concentrate it even more, and we have a laser that can cut through sheet metal. As Jesus said, "I will put together my church, a church so expansive with energy that not even the gates of hell will be able to keep it out" (Matthew 16:18 *The Message*).

Have you ever thought of the church this way? That it's the heart of God's plan and the hope of the world? That it's the most

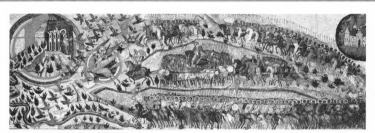

Figure 8.3. The militant church, a Russian icon from the sixteenth century A.D.

dynamic, active, vibrant, forceful project on the planet? That it is the one thing we will give our lives to that will live on long after we are gone—and not just for a generation or two, but for all of eternity?

You should.

As Bill Hybels so eloquently writes,

> It's the power of the love of Jesus Christ, the love that conquers sin and wipes out shame and heals wounds and reconciles enemies and patches broken dreams and ultimately changes the world, one life at a time. And the radical message of that transforming love has been given to the church.

Which is why the church is the most beautiful, the most radical, the most dangerous, the most glorious enterprise on the planet, and there is nothing more worthy of throwing our lives into.

As Bill continues:

> There is nothing like the local church when it's working
> right. Its beauty is indescribable. Its power is breathtak-
> ing. Its potential is unlimited. It comforts the grieving and
> heals the broken in the context of community. It builds
> bridges to seekers and offers truth to the confused. It pro-
> vides resources for those in need and opens its arms to the
> forgotten, the downtrodden, the disillusioned. It breaks
> the chains of addictions, frees the oppressed, and offers
> belonging to the marginalized of this world. Whatever the
> capacity for human suffering, the church has a greater ca-
> pacity for healing and wholeness.

The church does not have a mission. No, there *is a mission—
and it has the church.* And we're either in or out, signed up or on
the margins, on the field or on the sidelines, active or passive.
And our choice matters. There is an old tale, supposedly told by
Erasmus, which tells of when Jesus returned to heaven after his
time on earth. The angels gathered around him to learn what
had happened. Jesus told them of his miracles, his teaching and
his death and resurrection. When he finished, the archangel
Michael asked, "But Lord, what happens now?"

Jesus answered, "I have left behind eleven faithful men who
will declare my message and express my love. These faithful
men will establish and build my church. And that church will
take my message, my life, to the world."

"But," responded Michael, "What if they fail? What then?"

Jesus answered, "I have no other plan."

UNHINDERED

A word has captivated me for over twenty-five years, ever since
I first stumbled upon its significance while studying Greek in

seminary. It's *unhindered*. If something is "hindered," it's held back, kept back, restrained. Something has gotten in the way, prevented it, stopped it. If something is *unhindered*, it is set free. It advances. It goes forward.

Unhindered has loomed large in my thinking for so long because of its unique place in the New Testament, and particularly in the book of Acts. The word is used twenty-five times in the New Testament, seven times in the book of Acts alone. Acts is a book about Jesus' gospel going through barrier after barrier as it breaks out into the world and into the hearts of men and women. It's about the church overcoming roadblocks and impediments, persecutions and trials as it grows and boldly proclaims Christ. And it's about individuals who will not allow anything to stop them from being used by God to take Christ to the world.

Let's take a quick tour.

In the eighth chapter of Acts we find a young man who was head of the Queen of Ethiopia's treasury. He had been to Jerusalem and was reading a portion of the book of Isaiah in his chariot. We don't know anything of his background, only that something had urged him to explore the Old Testament and the faith of Abraham, Isaac and Jacob. The Holy Spirit urged Philip, one of the apostles, to approach the eunuch and ask if he understood what he was reading. The eunuch said, "How can I, unless someone guides me?" So Philip explained how the prophecies of the Old Testament told of a coming Messiah, and that Jesus was that Messiah. But that wasn't all:

> And as they were going along the road they came to some water, and the eunuch said, "See, here is water! What prevents me from being baptized?" And he commanded the chariot to stop, and they both went down into the water,

Philip and the eunuch, and he baptized him. (Acts 8:31, 36-38 ESV)

In the Greek, "What prevents me from being baptized" literally reads "What hinders me?" And the answer is *nothing.* This was a Jew witnessing to an Ethiopian. Crossing racial, ethnic, political boundaries.

The gospel was going out to the world.

Then comes Acts 10.

Peter was given a vision that he should no longer be bound by Jewish dietary rules, that under Christ, the law had been fulfilled, symbolic of the gospel going not only to the Jews but also the Gentiles. Just after that dream, the Holy Spirit prompted Peter to visit a man named Cornelius who had asked for some time with him. Cornelius was not a Jew. He was a Roman centurion. At that time, it was against Jewish law for a Jew to associate with a Gentile or even to visit one. But the urging of the Spirit was clear. Do not show favoritism. All are to be accepted. All are to be reached.

So Peter went.

The centurion asked about Jesus. Peter told him, and Cornelius and his household gave their lives to Christ. But that's not all: "Then Peter said, 'Can anyone keep these people from being baptized with water? They have received the Holy Spirit just as we have.' So he ordered that they be baptized in the name of Jesus Christ" (Acts 10:47-48).

The sentence "Can anyone keep these people from being baptized" literally reads "Can anyone *hinder*" or "Can anyone *forbid*" or "Can anyone *stop*" this from happening? And the answer was no.

Now, we turn to Acts 11.

Some people didn't like what happened between Peter and

Cornelius. Apparently they hadn't got word yet about Philip and the Ethiopian, but this news had reached them quickly. In a hastily called meeting the church leaders asked Peter, "Is it true? You went to the house of a Gentile? You ate with him? And, and, you baptized him?" The idea of the gospel of Jesus exploding outside of Judaism into the Gentile world was mind-boggling. As disciples they knew that Jesus was God in human form come to earth to show the way, but they didn't quite get the scope of his mission. For them, he was the Messiah for the Jews. But that the Messiah was for the *world* was beyond their comprehension. Yes, Jesus crossed some pretty radical boundaries—there was, after all, that scene with the Samaritan woman at the well, and Zacchaeus was a bit sketchy—but did Jesus mean to unleash all this? Did he really come for *everyone?* Everywhere? So they took Peter to task, and Peter replied:

> "As I began to speak, the Holy Spirit came on them as he had come on us at the beginning. Then I remembered what the Lord had said: 'John baptized with water, but you will be baptized with the Holy Spirit.' So if God gave them the same gift as he gave us, who believed in the Lord Jesus Christ, who was I to think that I could oppose God?"
>
> When they heard this, they had no further objections and praised God, saying, "So then, God has granted even the Gentiles repentance unto life." (Acts 11:15-18)

There is our theme: *unhindered.*

But there is one passage that captures this dynamic, at least for me, more than any other. It brought *unhindered* to my attention so many years ago. In Acts 20 we pick up the end of Paul's life. He had become a controversial figure on a number of fronts, but the bottom line is that where Paul went, Christianity went, and where Christianity went, the world was being turned upside down. Religiously, culturally, economically. Quite literally, riots broke out.

Paul had been beaten with rods, stoned, robbed, imprisoned, flogged and lashed. Now the Holy Spirit strongly urged him to go to Jerusalem, which was not a place Paul should go. It was the hotbed of opposition to everything he was about, which is why he had avoided it for years. And he knew what awaited him there. He was under no illusions about what was ahead:

> And now, compelled by the Spirit, I am going to Jerusalem, not knowing what will happen to me there. I only know that in every city the Holy Spirit warns me that prison and hardships are facing me. However, I consider my life worth nothing to me, if only I may finish the race and complete the task the Lord Jesus has given me—the task of testifying to the gospel of God's grace. (Acts 20:22-24)

The Scriptures go on to say that those who heard him wept, embraced and kissed him, and prayed with him. But then it was on to Jerusalem. Every step of the way, people urged Paul to turn around. And the Holy Spirit made it clear what lay before him. Paul's journey to Jerusalem had taken him to Caesarea, where he was staying with Philip, the one who had baptized the Ethiopian official. While there, according to Luke, Paul had a visitor:

> A prophet named Agabus came down from Judea. Coming over to us, he took Paul's belt, tied his own hands and feet with it and said, "The Holy Spirit says, 'In this way the Jews of Jerusalem will bind the owner of this belt and will hand him over to the Gentiles.'" (Acts 21:10-11)

How's that for an incentive! God urges Paul to do something, he obeys, and then God sends a prophet to say, "Now, are you sure you want to do this? Because here's the deal: You'll be betrayed by your own, hog-tied, and then handed over to your enemies. Who knows what they'll do to you? Just wanted to make sure you got those details down when you MapQuested the trip."

And how did those close to Paul respond? Just the way you'd think: "When we heard this, we and the people there pleaded with Paul not to go up to Jerusalem" (Acts 21:12).

How did Paul respond?

> Then Paul answered, "Why are you weeping and breaking my heart? I am ready not only to be bound, but also to die in Jerusalem for the name of the Lord Jesus." When he would not be dissuaded, we gave up and said, "The Lord's will be done." (Acts 21:13-14)

So what happened with Paul?

We don't know exactly. We *do* know that he went to Jerusalem, was arrested by the Jewish leaders under false pretences, and during that arrest they tried to kill him. Some Roman officers broke it up and then bound Paul in chains and arrested him for inciting a riot. As they began to flog him for good measure, Paul told them that he was a Roman citizen, which was true. That meant he had to be released and stand trial. But the city was so embroiled that they had to put him in protective custody. There the Holy Spirit urged him to take his case all the way to Rome so he could proclaim Christ there too.

He was first taken to Felix, the governor of Judea, where the Jews tried to make their case that Paul should be killed. Paul was too controversial, so Felix simply waited. Eventually, after two years, Felix was replaced by Festus. After the inauguration, Felix said, "By the way, you have this guy named Paul in prison. Good luck." Only three days after Festus arrived, the Jewish leaders showed up to make their case against Paul. They wanted Paul transferred to Jerusalem for trial, where they planned to kill him. Paul once again exercised his right as a Roman citizen and appealed directly to Caesar. So Paul was sent to Rome. After a storm, a shipwreck, a snakebite and a few other encouraging events, Paul arrived in Rome, where he was put under house arrest until his trial.

That is all we know.

Acts ends with Paul still in Rome, after two years, awaiting his time before Caesar. After that, we do not know what happened. There is some indication he had his trial, was able to proclaim Christ throughout Rome, was released and traveled to Greece to continue his efforts. One tradition says he also journeyed to Spain. If he was released, which is not certain, he apparently was arrested again in Rome by Nero, where there is every indication that he was executed. Tradition says he was beheaded. There is a church on the outskirts of Rome that claims to be built over his burial site.

We *do* know, however, that through his obedience he not only brought the message of Christ to Rome but while in Rome he wrote some of the most pivotal portions of the New Testament, including Ephesians, Philippians, Colossians, Philemon and later, possibly under Nero's imprisonment, 2 Timothy.

But the book of Acts ends with Paul in Rome.

However, that's not the *final* word. And I mean that literally. The final verses of Acts say: "For two whole years Paul stayed there in his own rented house and welcomed all who came to see him. Boldly and without hindrance he preached the kingdom of God and taught about the Lord Jesus Christ" (Acts 28:30-31). In Greek, the adverb is placed at the very end. Though it's a bit awkward when put directly into English, it reads that Paul was "proclaiming the kingdom of God and teaching the things concerning the Lord Jesus Christ with all boldness un-hinderedly." And that's the last word of the last chapter in the book of Acts.

Unhindered.

From the Jews to the Gentiles; from Jerusalem to Rome.

And from Rome to today.

AFTERWORD

Soon after my appointment to the presidency of Gordon-Conwell Theological Seminary, I received a phone call inviting my wife, Susan, and me to a visit with Billy and Ruth Graham at their home in the Blue Ridge mountains of Montreat, North Carolina. Billy had been instrumental in the establishment of the school, along with Harold Ockenga and J. Howard Pew, and I was to be only the fourth president in the school's already storied history.

As Susan and I were escorted to their rustic mountain retreat, past the old moonshiner's cabin Ruth chose to keep intact from earlier owners, we discovered we were in store for more than an afternoon with a man and a woman who had been used by God to influence the wider evangelical world more than any other figures in the twentieth century.

We were in store for some living history.

Billy began to reminisce, telling stories. I asked him for the founding vision of the seminary and the many other institutions that he helped shape: *Christianity Today* magazine, Fuller Theologi-

Figure A.1. Reverend Billy Graham

cal Seminary, Wheaton College, the National Association of Evangelicals, the Lausanne movement and more. The vision for each was the same. As he began his world travels, Billy found that Christians around the world did not know one another, and he felt God impress his heart to bring them together. That, he said, was one of the principal reasons he wanted to see such institutions founded. There needed to be a place where evangelicals could get to know one another, be brought together, build relationships and form the alliances needed to affect the world for Christ. Fragmented, they would not have the synergy and strength needed to bring the gospel to bear on the world. At the peak of Billy's influence, the great need was to network likeminded Christians around the world for the Great Commission. In so many ways Billy's efforts succeeded. Christians were brought together and the world was deeply affected.

As we drove away, I couldn't help but think about Billy's vision for Christians around the world, and how at the end of his life so much that he labored to achieve was in peril. Once again, evangelical Christians are in need of a unifying vision and a common foundation to stand upon. The core issues remain the same. Now, though, the problem is less organizational than theological, less networking than soul-searching, less programmatic than strategic. Billy brought the evangelical world together through four deep convictions: he believed in truth and the truth of the Bible; he was passionate about evangelism and doing everything possible to effectively reach out to a fallen world; he modeled civility and love toward others; and he believed deeply in the centrality of the church. Whether self-consciously or not, these were precisely the four pillars around which evangelical faith has been gathered throughout Christian history.

We need to coalesce around them again.

There is more that could be said of that day. Billy, using his walker, showed me around the house that Ruth had almost single-handedly filled with odds and ends found at yard sales and auctions. My time there ended with him taking me into his study, where he had written his sermons for the crusades that reached millions. Littered throughout were pictures of family and people who had influenced his life—all now gone to be with the God they had given their lives to serve.

I was touched, as so many have been before me, by his humility and genuine grace. But even more by his passionate love for Ruth, who sadly passed away just a few months after our visit. Following an hour or so of conversation, he walked us back to the bedroom where Ruth was confined. She had gamely prepared to receive us and had been moved to a nearby chair, next to a low-lying bookshelf where notebooks containing books of the Bible had been prepared for her with oversized type so that she could read them despite her failing eyesight. Billy and Ruth talked of their nightly devotions together, how they prayed for their children, and how those who said there was no romance at their age were wrong. "We have romance through our eyes," Billy explained.

He was right. They did.

He seemed far more honored to entertain us in his home than we were to be entertained. He insisted on walking us to the door and stood waving at our car until we were out of sight down the steep mountain road.

This book is my small way of waving back.

NOTES

Introduction

p. 12   "They don't have a natural presidential candidate": David D. Kirkpatrick, "The Evangelical Crackup," *New York Times Magazine*, October 28, 2007, cover.

p. 13   The evangelical mosaic is still united in its efforts: Charles Colson, "The Demise of the Religious Right?" *Breakpoint*, October 30, 2007.

p. 13   growing divide "over the evangelical alliance": Kirkpatrick, "The Evangelical Crackup," p. 40.

p. 13   young Americans don't know Billy Graham: "Go Figure," Christianity Today, October 30, 2007 <www.christianitytoday .com/ct/2007/november/12.18.html>.

pp. 13-14 "Meanwhile, a younger generation of evangelical pastors": Kirkpatrick, "The Evangelical Crackup," p. 40.

p. 16   conversionism, activism, biblicism, and crucicentrism: David W. Bebbington, *Evangelicalism in Modern Britain: A History from the 1730s to the 1980s* (Boston: Unwin Hyman, 1989).

p. 16   "a quadrilateral of priorities": Ibid., p. 3.

p. 16   while "reliance on Scripture remains": Mark A. Noll, *American Evangelical Christianity: An Introduction* (Oxford: Blackwell, 2001), pp. 24-25.

p. 16   atonement is the center of heated theological discourse: For example, see Scot McKnight, *A Community Called Atonement* (Nashville: Abingdon, 2007).

p. 17   the singular personality and presence of Billy Graham: The two best books on Billy Graham are William Martin's *A Prophet with Honor: The Billy Graham Story* (New York: William Morrow, 1991), and Billy's own autobiography, *Just As I Am: The Autobiography of Billy Graham* (New York: HarperSanFrancisco/Zondervan, 1997).

p. 18   "the silent creep of impending doom": Jim Collins, *How the Mighty Fall* (New York: Harper Collins, 2009), p. 1.

p. 19   "rise of the rest": Fareed Zakaria, *The Post-American World* (New York: W. W. Norton, 2008).

Chapter 1: Truthiness

p. 23   "signs of ideas": See Aristotle's *De Interpretatione* 16a3-8. Thomas Aquinas took this section of Aristotle's thought and summarized it as "words are but the signs of ideas" (see Mortimer J. Adler, *How to Think About the Great Ideas* [Chicago: Open Court, 2000], p. 291).

p. 24   "And that brings us to tonight's word": Stephen Colbert, *The Colbert Report*, October 17, 2005 < www.colbertnation.com/the-colbert-report-videos/24039/october-17-2005/the-word---truthiness>. See also "Colbert's 'Truthiness' Strikes a Chord," *USA Today*, August 28, 2006, p. 1D.

p. 24   "*Truthiness* is the bald assertion that": " 'Podcast' Is the Word of the Year," *Yahoo! Financial News*, December 5, 2005 <http://biz.yahoo.com/prnews/051205/nym208.html?.v=26>; "New Words of 2005," National Public Radio *Morning Edition*, December 30, 2005. Audio file of the report <www.npr.org/templates/story/story.php?storyId=5075545>.

pp. 24-26   *wikiality*: Stephen Colbert, *The Colbert Report*, July 31, 2006 <www.colbertnation.com/the-colbert-report-videos/72347/july-31-2006/the-word---wikiality?videoId=72347>.

p. 25   Wikipedia is one of the Web's most popular destinations: Brock Read, " 'Wikimania' Participants Give the Online Encyclopedia Mixed Reviews," *Chronicle of Higher Education,* September 1, 2006, p. A62.

p. 26   "Together we can create a reality": Stephen Colbert, *The Colbert Report,* July 31, 2006 <www.colbertnation.com/the-colbert-report-videos/72347/july-31-2006/the-word---wikiality?videoId=72347>.

p. 26   "*two plus two does equal five*": Marshall Poe, "The Hive," *The Atlantic*, September 2006.

p. 27   "We wanted to produce a report": Cornelia Dean, "Evolution Book Sees No Science-Religion Gap," *New York Times*, January 4, 2008, p. A11 <www.nytimes.com/2008/01/04/us/04evolve.html>.

p. 27   "attempts to pit science and religion against each other": Committee on Revising Science and Creationism, "Science, Evolution and Creationism," National Academy of Sciences and Institute of Medicine of the National Academies. Available as a free PDF at <http://cart.nap.edu/cart/deliver.cgi?record_id=11876>.

p. 28   "Nothing has come to characterize modern science": Ronald L. Numbers, "Science Without God: Natural Laws and Christian Beliefs," in *When Science and Christianity Meet*, ed. David C. Lindberg and Ronald L. Numbers (Chicago: University of Chicago Press, 2003), p. 265.

p. 31   Jews as an "erosion of capital" and a "waste of space": Laurence Rees, *Auschwitz: A New History* (New York: Public Affairs, 2005), p. 37.

p. 31   the removal of "lebensunwertes Leben": Ibid., p. 176.

p. 31   Jews as gangrenous appendixes: Ibid., p. 177.

p. 32   "He draws back the curtain to reveal": William Hendricks, *A Theology for Children* (Nashville: Broadman & Holman, 1980), p. 41.

p. 34   Hebrew mind is concerned with what a thing is for, and does it work: For a good introduction to the Hebrew mindset, see Marvin R. Wilson, *Our Father Abraham* (Grand Rapids: Eerdmans, 1989).

pp. 37-38   "You must be home before eleven": Lee Strobel, *Inside the Mind of Unchurched Harry and Mary* (Grand Rapids: Zondervan, 1993), pp. 115-16.

pp. 38-39   Adam McKay and Will Farrell, *Talladega Nights: The Ballad of Ricky Bobby*, Sony Pictures, 2006 <www.sonypictures.com/previews/player/homevideo/talladeganights/index.html>. Click on "Dinner Table."

p. 39   *A Million Little Pieces*: Richard N. Ostling, "Latest Question in Culture Wars: What Is Truth?" Associated Press, January 24, 2006; "A Million Little Lies," *The Smoking Gun*, January 8, 2006 <www.thesmokinggun.com/jamesfrey/0104061jamesfrey1.html>; Hillel Italie, "Oprah Confronts Author on Live Show," *Charlotte Observer*, January 27, 2006, p. 3A.

p. 40   "it were really a matter of indifference": Sigmund Freud, cited in "Truth," in *The Great Ideas: A Syntopicon of Great Books of the Western World*, ed. Mortimer J. Adler (Chicago: Encyclopedia Britannica, Inc., 1952), p. 915.

p. 41   Billy Graham's prayer: Billy Graham, quoted in William Martin, *A Prophet with Honor: The Billy Graham Story* (New York: William Morrow, 1991), p. 112.

p. 42   Graham says that single resolution: Ibid.

p. 42   Chuck Templeton left the faith: Lee Strobel, *The Case for Faith* (Grand Rapids: Zondervan, 2000), p. 18.

Chapter 2: Orthodoxy

pp. 44-45   "Shibboleth rattled around in my head": Richard Dorment, "Doris Slacedo: A Glimpse into the Abyss," London *Telegraph*, October 9, 2007 <http://www.telegraph.co.uk>. To see images of the *Shibboleth,* please visit <www.tate.org.uk/modern/ exhibitions/dorissalcedo/photos.shtm>.

p. 45   there is "truth to tell": Lesslie Newbigin, *Truth to Tell: The Gospel as Public Truth* (Grand Rapids: Eerdmans, 1991).

pp. 45-46   "General theories are everywhere condemned": G. K. Chesterton, *Heretics* (Peabody, Mass.: Hendrickson, 2007), p. 2.

p. 47   "calling people into trustworthy community": Tony Jones, an email from Emergent Village on why they do not and will not have an emergent statement of faith. See also Tony Jones, *The New Christians: Dispatches from the Emergent Frontier* (San Francisco: Jossey-Bass, 2008), pp. 233-35.

p. 47   "It is not enthusiasm, but dogma": T. S. Eliot, *Christianity and Culture* (San Diego: Harcourt Brace & Co., 1976), p. 47.

p. 48   Brother and sister sexual trysts: Joan McFadden, "I Used to Have Sex with My Brother but I Don't Feel Guilty About It," London *Times*, July 15, 2008, pp. 10-11 <http://women.times online.co.uk/tol/life_and_style/women/families/article4332635 .ece>.

pp. 48-49   The rights of chimps: Jeffrey Stinson, "Activists Pursue Basic Legal Rights for Great Apes," *USA Today International*, July 16, 2008, p. 2A <www.usatoday.com/news/offbeat/2008-07-15- chimp_N.htm>.

p. 49   "Every plank in the platform of orthodoxy": Bruce Shelley, *Church History in Plain Language*, 2nd ed. (Nashville: Thomas Nelson, 1995), p. 48.

p. 50   Jeffrey Burton Russell's thesis: Jeffrey Burton Russell, *A History of Medieval Christianity: Prophecy and Order* (Arlington Heights, Ill.: Harland Davidson, 1968).

p. 50   "The search for order and the urge to prophecy": Ibid., p. 6.

p. 50   The meaning of *orthodoxy:* The Orthodox Churches, such as the Greek Orthodox Church, is always spelled with a capital *O.* The orthodoxy I speak of here is spelled with a lowercase *o.*

p. 52   from *sin* to *crime* to *sickness:* Karl Menninger, *Whatever Became of Sin?* (New York: Hawthorn, 1973).

p. 53   vanishing Christian words: James Tozer, "Is It a Sin? Christian Words Deleted from Oxford Dictionary," *Daily Mail*, December 7, 2008 <www.dailymail.co.uk/news/article-1092668/Is-sin-Christian-words-deleted-Oxford-dictionary.html#>.

p. 53   "Christianity is either degenerating into a pathetic version": Christian Smith, *Soul Searching: The Religious and Spiritual Lives of American Teenagers* (Oxford: Oxford University Press, 2005), p. 171.

p. 54   "They are rage shootings": Greg Toppo, "10 Years Later, the Real Story Behind Columbine," *USA Today*, April 14, 2009, pp. 1A-2A. Link to story: <www.usatoday.com/news/nation/2009-04-13-columbine-myths_N.htm?se=yahoorefer&poe=HFMost Popular&loc=interstitialskip>; Greg Toppo and Marilyn Elias, "Lessons from Columbine," *USA Today*, April 14, 2009, pp. 1D-2D <www.usatoday.com/news/education/2009-04-13-columbine-lessons_N.htm>.

pp. 54-55   The loss of the American dream: Ted Anthony, "Why Are Americans Killing Each Other?" *Charlotte Observer,* Sunday, April 5, 2009 <www.charlotteobserver.com/408/story/644582.html>.

p. 55   In truth, he chose to, he *wanted* to: Ron Rosenbaum, *Explaining Hitler: The Search for the Origins of His Evil* (New York: Random House, 1998).

p. 55   when we have lost the term *evil:* Jean Bethke Elshtain, *Evangelicals in the Public Square*, ed. J. Budziszewski (Grand Rapids: Baker Academic, 2006), p. 204.

pp. 57-58   Chesterton's lamppost analogy: G. K. Chesterton, *G. K. Chesterton: Essential Writings*, ed. William Griffin (Maryknoll, N.Y.: Orbis, 2003), p. 57.

pp. 58-59   History of "mere Christian": Alan Jacobs, *The Narnian: The Life and Imagination of C. S. Lewis* (New York: HarperSanFrancisco, 2005), pp. 213-14.

pp. 59-60   The hall and the rooms analogy: C. S. Lewis, *Mere Christianity* (New York: Macmillan, 1943, 1945, 1952), p. xi.

p. 61   *Veritas Christo et ecclesiae:* On the history of the founding of Harvard, see "New England's First Fruits" (1640), Constitution Society <www.constitution.org/primarysources/firstfruits.html>.

pp. 61-62   "preachers insist too much upon doctrine": Dorothy L. Sayers,

"The Greatest Drama Ever Staged," in *The Whimsical Christian*
(New York: Collier, 1978), p. 11.

Chapter 3: The World Without Us

p. 65   "The notion is not that the world is tasteless": John R. W. Stott,
               Christian Counter Culture (Downers Grove, Ill.: InterVarsity
               Press, 1978), p. 59.

p. 66   Culture as "webs of significance": Clifford Geertz, *The Interpre-
               tation of Cultures* (New York: Basic Books, 1973), esp. "Thick
               Description: Toward an Interpretive Theory of Culture," pp.
               3-30.

p. 67   Niebuhr's typologies: H. Richard Niebuhr, *Christ and Culture*
               (New York: Harper & Row, 1951).

p. 67   Niebuhr on how Christ and culture compete: See D. A. Carson,
               Christ and Culture Revisited (Grand Rapids: Eerdmans, 2008);
               and Craig A. Carter, *Rethinking Christ and Culture* (Grand Rap-
               ids: Brazos, 2006).

p. 67   "American culture has triumphed": Alan Wolfe, *The Transfor-
               mation of American Culture: How We Actually Live Our Faith*
               (New York: Free Press, 2003), p. 3.

p. 68   "changes to our method": David Wells, "Satanism, Starbucks,
               and Other Gospel Challengers," *9Marks,* July/August 2007
               <http://www.9marks.org/ejournal/satanism-starbucks-and-
               other-gospel-challengers>.

p. 71   "When He moves, revival will come": Leonard Ravenhill, *Why
               Revival Tarries* (Minneapolis: Bethany, 1959), p. 139.

p. 71   "wee shall be as a Citty upon a Hill": John Winthrop, *A Modell
               of Christian Charity* (1630), quoted in Conrad Cherry, *God's
               New Israel: Religious Interpretations of American Destiny* (Engle-
               wood Cliffs, N.J.: Prentice-Hall, 1971), p. 43.

p. 71   "the essence of America's motivating mythology": Cherry, *God's
               New Israel*, p. vii.

p. 72   America was *not* founded as a Christian nation: Mark A. Noll,
               Nathan O. Hatch and George M. Marsden, *The Search for Chris-
               tian America*, 2nd ed. (Colorado Springs: Helmers & Howard,
               1989).

p. 73   "Jesus loves porn stars": See "Jesus Loves Porn Stars," XXX-
               Church.com <http://triplexchurch.com/_pdf/jlps2009.pdf>.

pp. 73-74   "GLBTQ can live lives in accord with biblical Christianity":
               Tony Jones, cited in "Tony Jones Blesses Gay Marriage and Or-

dination," ChristianityToday.com, November 26, 2008 <www .outofur.com/archives/2008/11/tony_jones_bles.html>.

p. 74   celebrification of our culture: See Joseph Epstein, "Celebrity Culture," *The Hedgehog Review: Critical Reflections on Contemporary Culture* 7, no. 1 (2005).

pp. 74-75   "our culture values only two things": Ibid., p. 14.

p. 75   "No issue or idea in our culture can gain any traction": Jennifer L. Geddes, "An Interview with Richard Schickel," *The Hedgehog Review: Critical Reflections on Contemporary Culture* 7, no. 1 (2005): p. 82.

p. 75   "Cultural Awareness: Following Bono": From Emergent-See Po-Motivators <www.spurgeon.org/~phil/posters.htm>.

p. 76   our goal is not cultural transformation: Mark Galli, "On Not Transforming the World," ChristianityToday.com, August 9, 2007 <www.christianitytoday.com/ct/2007/augustweb-only/132-42.0 .html?start=1>.

p. 76   the practice of making culture: Andy Crouch, *Culture Making* (Downers Grove, Ill.: InterVarsity Press, 2008).

p. 76   "compelling artistic and intellectual works": James Davison Hunter, "Transforming the Culture," *Image*, November 2006.

p. 76   Our tools for such an effort have never changed: John Stott, *The Living Church* (Downers Grove, Ill.: InterVarsity Press, 2007), pp. 135-38.

p. 77   "It is not enough simply to see the evil": T. S. Eliot, *Christianity and Culture* (New York: Harcourt Brace, 1967), p. 75.

p. 78   "God's extension of favor to all people": Stanley J. Grenz, David Guretzki, and Cherith Fee Nordling, *Pocket Dictionary of Theological Terms* (Downers Grove, Ill.: InterVarsity Press, 1999), p. 56.

p. 78   "Common grace is evident in the divine government": Philip Edgcumbe Hughes, "Grace," in *Evangelical Dictionary of Theology*, ed. Walter Elwell, 2nd ed. (Grand Rapids: Baker, 2001), pp. 519-22.

pp. 78-79   "Understanding Christianity as a worldview is important": Charles Colson and Nancy Pearcey, *How Now Shall We Live?* (Wheaton, Ill.: Tyndale House, 1999), p. 33.

p. 81   Beauty is often the first to lose its moorings: For an excellent introduction to the role of art in relation to culture, see H. R. Rookmaaker, *Modern Art and the Death of a Culture* (Wheaton, Ill.: Crossway, 1994).

Chapter 4: Of Tabernacles and Mosques

p. 84   Metrosexual identity: I recall gathering some of these "descrip-
                 tors" from some rather generic article on metrosexuals, but
                 cannot recall the source.

p. 85   "religious emotion divorced from religious belief": Christopher
                 Dawson, *Dynamics of World History,* ed. John Molloy (Wil-
                 mington, Del.: ISI Books, 2002), p. 103.

pp. 85-86   "the challenge to Christianity": For a summary of the ARIS
                 study, along with links to the full survey, see Barry A. Kosmin
                 and Ariela Keysar, "American Religious Identity Survey 2008"
                 <www.americanreligionsurvey-aris.org>.

p. 86   "These people aren't secularized": Barry A. Kosmin, quoted in
                 Cathy Lee Grossman, "Almost All Denominations Losing
                 Ground," *USA Today,* March 9, 2009, p. 1A, 6A.

p. 86   Unbelief has become more readily available: James Turner,
                 Without God, Without Creed (Baltimore: Johns Hopkins Univer-
                 sity Press, 1985), p. 262.

p. 86   "A couple came in to my office": Quoted in Grossman, "Almost
                 All Denominations Losing Ground," p. 6A.

p. 86   "I really have never thought about that": Quoted in Phil Zuck-
                 erman, *Society Without God* (New York: New York University
                 Press, 2008). See also Peter Steinfels, "A Land of Nonbelievers,
                 Which Is Not to Say Atheists," *New York Times,* February 28,
                 2009, p. A15.

p. 86   "If India is the most religious country on our planet": Peter
                 Berger, et al., *Religious America, Secular Europe* (Burlington, Vt.:
                 Ashgate, 2009), p. 12.

p. 87   Southern Baptist decline: Southern Baptist churches baptized
                 fewer people in 2008 for the fourth year in a row to reach the
                 lowest level since 1987, and membership in the country's larg-
                 est Protestant denomination fell as well, according to an an-
                 nual report released Thursday, April 23, 2009, cited in "Our
                 World," *Charlotte Observer,* April 25, 2009, p. 4A.

p. 89   "We do violence to the poor": John Green, quoted in an un-
                 signed editorial, "The Greatest Social Need," *Christianity To-
                 day,* January 19, 2009.

p. 91   total population of the world: "U.S. and World Population
                 Clocks," U.S. Census Bureau <www.census.gov/main/www/
                 popclock.html>.

pp. 91-92   Most non-Christians do not know a Christian: Todd Johnson and Charles L. Tieszen, "Personal Contact: The Sine Qua Non of Twenty-First Century Christian Mission," *Evangelical Missions Quarterly*, October 2007.

p. 92   "Let not a man associate with the wicked": *Mekilta de Rabbi Ishmael*, tractate *Amalek* 3.55-57 on Exodus 18:1, as cited by Darrell L. Bock, *Luke* (Grand Rapids: Baker, 1996), 2:1299.

p. 95   "Outsiders believe Christians do not like them": David Kinnaman and Gabe Lyons, *unChristian: What a New Generation Really Thinks About Christianity* (Grand Rapids: Baker, 2007), p. 27.

p. 96   "I certainly hope that Hillary is the candidate": Jerry Falwell, quoted in "Hating Hillary," *Christianity Today*, March 3, 2008 <www.christianitytoday.com/ct/2008/march/14.26.html>.

p. 96   Niemoller's dream about Hitler: Tony Campolo, *Let Me Tell You a Story* (Nashville: Word, 2000), p. 108.

p. 98   "The line separating good and evil": Aleksandr Solzhenitsyn, *The Gulag Archipelago* (New York: Harper & Row, 1973).

pp. 99-100   Gift of a Gideon New Testament: Penn Jillette, "Penn Says: A Gift of a Bible," *Crackle*, December 8, 2008 <http://crackle.com/c/Penn_Says/A_Gift_of_a_Bible/2415037>.

Chapter 5: The Mark of a Christian

pp. 101-2   "argument culture": Deborah Tannen, *The Argument Culture* (New York: Random House, 1998).

p. 102   The lack of civility in our world: Janet Kornblum, "Rudeness, Threats Make the Web a Cruel World," *USA Today*, July 31, 2007, pp. 1A, 2A; "Defending Wikipedia's Impolite Side," Noam Cohen, *New York Times*, Monday, August 20, 2007, p. C3.

p. 102   "anger in America": Peter Wood, *A Bee in the Mouth: Anger in America Now* (New York: Encounter Books, 2006).

p. 103   "self-appointed attack dogs of Christendom": David Aikman, "Attack Dogs of Christendom," *Christianity Today*, August 2007, p. 52.

p. 104   "Churches have too many problems": See James Emery White, *Rethinking the Church* (Grand Rapids: Baker, 2003), pp. 21-22.

p. 104   "Dear Lord, bless the man": Bob Jones Sr., quoted in William Martin, *A Prophet with Honor: The Billy Graham Story* (New York: William Morrow, 1991), p. 318.

p. 105   "We rush in, being very, very pleased": Francis Schaeffer, *The Great Evangelical Disaster* (Westchester, Ill.: Crossway, 1984), p. 174.

p. 106   they shared the gospel like it was gossip: Michael Green, *Evan-
              gelism in the Early Church* (Grand Rapids: Eerdmans, 1970), p.
              173.

p. 106   "See how they love one another": Tertullian, *Apology* (A.D. 197).

p. 108   "Jesus is giving a right to the world": Francis Schaeffer, *The
              Mark of the Christian* (Downers Grove, Ill.: InterVarsity Press,
              1976), p. 161.

p. 108   Lovemarks, the "future beyond brands": "About Lovemarks,"
              Lovemarks <www.lovemarks.com/index.php?pageID=20020>;
              see also Kevin Roberts, *Lovemarks: The Future Beyond Brands*
              (Brooklyn, N.Y.: PowerHouse Books, 2004); and *The Lovemarks
              Effect: Winning in the Consumer Revolution* (Brooklyn, N.Y.:
              PowerHouse Books, 2006).

p. 109   a "stench that the world can smell": Schaeffer, *Mark of the Chris-
              tian*, p. 170.

p. 110   In truth, it is second-degree murder: In no way should the ex-
              ploration of second-degree murder in the context of this com-
              mandment be fully equated with first-degree murder. This runs
              the risk of eisegesis and can water down the meaning of the
              word *murder* itself. On this, see Joy Davidman, *Smoke on the
              Mountain* (Philadelphia: Westminster Press, 1953), pp. 77-78.

p. 110   "I don't hate anybody": Will D. Campbell, *Brother to a Dragon-
              fly* (New York: Continuum, 1987), p. 181.

p. 111   It's an assault with the intent to kill: See Bill Hybels, *Laws That
              Liberate* (Wheaton, Ill.: Victor, 1985), p. 74.

p. 111   Solomon Islanders yelling at trees: Adapted from Robert Ful-
              ghum, *All I Really Need to Know I Learned in Kindergarten* (New
              York: Villard Books, 1989), pp. 19-20.

p. 111   "rabies of the heart": Herman Melville, quoted in Os Guinness,
              *Steering Through Chaos: Vice and Virtue in an Age of Moral Con-
              fusion*, ed. Virginia Mooney (Colorado Springs: NavPress,
              2000), p. 71.

p. 112   The classic pattern of envy: Cornelius Plantinga Jr., *Not the Way
              It's Supposed to Be* (Grand Rapids: Eerdmans, 1995), p. 167.

pp. 112-13   The devils and the hermit: Adapted from Hesketh Pearson, *Os-
              car Wilde: His Life and Wit* (New York: Harper & Brothers,
              1946), pp. 127-28.

p. 115   Christianity's unique contribution: Philip Yancey, *What's So
              Amazing About Grace?* (Grand Rapids, Zondervan, 1997), p.
              45.

p. 115	God's love is unconditional: adapted from ibid., p. 45.
p. 118	"To be a Christian means to forgive the inexcusable": C. S. Lewis, "On Forgiveness," *The Weight of Glory* (New York: Collier, 1975), p. 125.
p. 119	Nietzsche's ability to "smell": See Yancey, *What's So Amazing About Grace?* p. 280.

Chapter 6: Polarizations

pp. 120-21	"Die, heretic!": Emo Philips, quoted in *GQ*, June 1999, p. 251; see also "GQ's Top 75 Jokes of All Time," EmoPhilips.com <www.emophilips.com/content/pdf/75-jokes.pdf>.
p. 121	"Why is it that so often in theological controversy": A. T. B. McGowan, ed., *Always Reforming: Explorations in Systematic Theology* (Downers Grove, Ill.: IVP Academic, 2006), p. 17.
p. 123	War as an option: Robert Corin Morris, "The Christians Are Fighting—Again," *Weavings* 22, no. 2 (2007): 24-32.
p. 123	Denominational statistics: World Christian Database <http://worldchristiandatabase.org/wcd/about/denominations.asp>.
pp. 123-24	Christmas on a Sunday: Rachel Zoll, "Some Megachurches Closing for Christmas," Associated Press, December 6, 2005 (http://www.religionnewsblog.com/12993); Frank E. Lockwood, "Why Do Churches Close on Sunday?" *Lexington Herald-Leader* (www.kentucky.com); Manya A. Brachear, "Evangelical Churches Such as Suburban Willow Creek Will Close on Christmas So Members Can Focus on Family," *Chicago Tribune*, December 6, 2005 (www.chicagotribune.com); Ken Garfield, "No Church Today; It's Christmas," *Charlotte Observer*, December 7, 2005 (www.charlotte.com); Laurie Goodstein, "When Christmas Falls on Sunday, Megachurches Take the Day Off," *New York Times*, December 9, 2005 (http://www.nytimes.com/2005/12/09/national/09church.html?_r=1); Skye Jethani, "Leader's Insight: Closed for Christmas," ChristianityToday.com.
p. 125	Calvinism "is potentially the most explosive and divisive issue": Steve Lemke, "The Future of Southern Baptists as Evangelicals," paper presented at the Maintaining Baptist Distinctives Conference, Mid-America Baptist Theological Seminary <www.nobts.edu/faculty/ItoR/LemkeSW/Personal/SBCfuture.pdf>.
p. 125	Calvin was "short-tempered and humorless": William Man-

chester, *A World Lit Only by Fire: The Medieval Mind and the Renaissance* (Boston: Little, Brown, 1992), p. 190.

p. 127   The village green: See Scot McKnight, "Who Are the Neo-Reformed?" *JesusCreed*, February 16, 2009 <http://blog.belief net.com/jesuscreed/2009/02/who-are-the-neoreformed.html>.

pp. 127-28   "Perhaps our criterion for deciding which is which": John Stott, *Evangelical Truth* (Downers Grove, Ill.: InterVarsity Press, 2005), p. 117.

p. 128   "In essentials, unity; in non-essentials, liberty; in all things, charity": Peter Meiderlin. As an external reader of this manuscript pointed out, this is commonly attributed to Augustine, though the phrase originated with Meiderlin. See Hans Rollmann, " 'In Essentials Unity': The Pre-History and History of a Restoration Movement Slogan," adapted from a lecture given at the Christian Scholars Conference, David Lipscomb University, July 1996.

p. 129   "It is dreadfully simple to dress up": McGowan, *Always Reforming*, p. 17.

p. 129   The proud of heart in hell: Dante Alighieri, *The Divine Comedy of Dante Alighieri*, Great Books of the Western World 21, ed. Robert Maynard Hutchins, trans. Charles Eliot Norton (Chicago: Encyclopaedia Britannica, 1952), p. 68.

p. 130   "he'll be so near the throne of God": John Wesley, Wesley Center for Applied Theology <http://wesley.nnu.edu/john_wesley/ methodist/chll.htm>.

p. 134   "To lick your wounds, to smack your lips": Frederick Buechner, *Wishful Thinking: A Theological ABC* (New York: Harper & Row, 1973), p. 2.

Chapter 7: Our Mother

pp. 137-38   leaders of evangelical Christianity disengaged from the church: D. Michael Lindsay, "A Gated Community in the Evangelical World," *USA Today*, February 11, 2008, p. 13A.

p. 138   expressing faith in God apart from the church: "Americans Embrace Various Alternatives to a Conventional Church Experience as Being Fully Biblical," *The Barna Update*, February 18, 2008 <www.barna.org/barna-update/article/19-organic-church /47-americans-embrace-various-alternatives-to-a-conventional -church-experience-as-being-fully-biblical>.

p. 139   "you act like there never was a Reformation": David Neff, "Together in the Jesus Story," *Christianity Today,* September 2006, p. 54.

p. 139 "stripped of our story": Kenneth Collins, *The Evangelical Moment: The Promise of an American Religion* (Grand Rapids: Baker Academic, 2005), p. 189.

p. 141 "right of common people to shape their own faith": Nathan Hatch, *The Democratization of American Christianity* (New Haven, Conn.: Yale University Press, 1989), p. 14.

p. 141 people had little if any sense of limitations: Ibid., pp. 9-11.

p. 142 the potential partnership of the church and parachurch: Wesley K. Wilmer, J. David Schmidt and Martyn Smith, *The Prospering Parachurch* (San Francisco: Jossey-Bass, 1998), p. xiv.

p. 143 Jim Bakker raised a lot of money: See Charles E. Shepard, *Forgiven: The Rise and Fall of Jim Bakker and the PTL Ministry* (New York: Atlantic Monthly Press, 1989), pp. 275-80.

p. 146 *one, holy, catholic* and *apostolic:* These marks were affirmed in the Niceno-Constantinopolitan Creed (A.D. 381).

p. 148 Christian church is confessional: I do not mean that churches should be part of the "Confessional Church," meaning those who adhere to the ancient confessions and creeds of the church and use them extensively in worship and teaching, but confessional in the most basic and simple of confessions.

p. 149 Formal confessions of faith: See Stanley J. Grenz, David Guretzki and Cherith Fee Nordling, *Pocket Dictionary of Theological Terms* (Downers Grove, Ill.: InterVarsity Press, 1999), p. 28. For a good introduction to such confessions, see Henry Bettenson and Chris Maunder, eds., *Documents of the Christian Church,* 3rd ed. (Oxford: Oxford University Press, 1999).

p. 149 The Creed of Nicaea: Bettenson and Maunder, *Documents,* p. 27.

p. 151 The mission of Christ creates the church: Jürgen Moltmann, *The Church in the Power of the Spirit* (New York: Harper & Row, 1977), p. 10. See also Darrell L. Guder, ed., *Missional Church* (Grand Rapids: Eerdmans, 1998).

p. 151 "our committed participation as God's people": Christopher J. H. Wright, *The Mission of God* (Downers Grove, Ill.: InterVarsity Press, 2006), pp. 22-23.

Chapter 8: The Church Unhindered

pp. 152-53 *Newsweek* article on the Republican party: "Your Mission: Resurrect the Republican Brand," *Newsweek,* December 29, 2008-January 5, 2009, p. 13.

p. 153   "when Paul made the cross the centerpiece": Sean McDonough,
            "Image Problem," *Every Thought Captive*, June 30, 2008 <http://
            connect.gordonconwell.edu/members/blog_view.asp?id=1900
            52&tag=Church+Image>.

p. 158   "We're disillusioned about almost everything": Katie Galli,
            "Dear Disillusioned Generation," ChristianityToday.com, April
            21, 2008 <www.christianitytoday.com/ct/2008/april/28.69
            .html>.

p. 159   "Christianity is not a purely intellectual, internal faith": Philip
            Yancey, *Church: Why Bother?* (Grand Rapids: Zondervan, 1998),
            p. 23.

p. 159   "I have been and continue to be frustrated": Sarah Cunning-
            ham, *Dear Church: Letters from a Disillusioned Generation*
            (Grand Rapids: Zondervan, 2006), p. 13.

p. 159   "search for the perfect church": Ibid., p. 42.

p. 160   seventies generation "were posers": Jean M. Twenge, *Genera-
            tion Me* (New York: Free Press, 2006), p. 1.

p, 160   "the culture of narcissism": Christopher Lasch, *The Culture of
            Narcissism* (New York: W. W. Norton, 1991).

pp. 161-62 "Salvation and church membership went together": John R. W.
            Stott, *The Living Church* (Downers Grove, Ill.: InterVarsity
            Press, 2007), p. 32.

p. 162   *ecclesia militans:* Richard A. Muller, *Dictionary of Latin and
            Greek Theological Terms* (Grand Rapids: Baker, 1985), pp. 99-
            100.

pp. 163-64 "There is nothing like the local church": Bill Hybels, *Coura-
            geous Leadership* (Grand Rapids: Zondervan, 2002), p. 21.

IMAGE CREDITS
AND PERMISSIONS